Live
CONSISTENTLY
When Life Goes Up and Down

Books by J. Allen Blair

Living Patiently—When God Seems Far Away
A Devotional Study of Job

Living Victoriously—When Winning It All Isn't Enough
A Devotional Study of Philippians

Living Peacefully—When the World Won't Leave You Alone
A Devotional Study of 1 Peter

Living Consistently—When Life Goes Up and Down
A Devotional Study of the Christian Life

Living CONSISTENTLY

When Life Goes Up and Down

A Devotional Study of the Christian Life

J. Allen Blair

kregel
PUBLICATIONS

Grand Rapids, MI 49501

Living Consistently—When Life Goes Up and Down
A Devotional Study of the Christian Life by J. Allen Blair.

Copyright © 1995 by J. Allen Blair.

Published in 1995 by Kregel Publications, a division of Kregel, Inc., P.O. Box 2607, Grand Rapids, MI 49501.

Cover Photograph: CLEO Photography
Cover and Book Design: Alan G. Hartman

Library of Congress Cataloging-in-Publication Data
Blair, J. Allen.
   [Profile of a Christian]
   Living consistently: when life goes up and down /
J. Allen Blair.
     p.   cm.
   Originally published: Profile of a Christian. Westchester.
Ill.: Good News Publishers, 1982.
   1. Christian life. I. Title.
BV4501.2.B5556   1995   248.4—dc20   94-38138
                                    CIP

ISBN 0-8254-2187-x (paperback)

1 2 3 4 5 Printing / Year 99 98 97 96 95

CONTENTS

PREFACE

If you have received Jesus Christ as your Savior and Lord, you have made the most important decision of your entire life. Those who have experienced this great salvation should be eternally grateful. Think what you were without Christ, but consider what you are by God's grace.

Paul reminded the Ephesians—and us—"And you hath he quickened, who were dead in trespasses and sins; Wherein in time past ye walked according to the course of this world, according to the prince of the power of the air, the spirit that now worketh in the children of disobedience: . . . God, who is rich in mercy, for his great love wherewith he loved us, Even when we were dead in sins, hath quickened us together with Christ, (by grace ye are saved;)" (Eph. 2:1–2, 4–5).

We were on our way to hell, and God in His mercy and love delivered us from the penalty and power of sin.

Following our salvation experience, we begin a journey that will eventually take us into the visible presence of Christ.

There is no promise that this journey will always be pleasant. There will be hardships, temptations, and sorrows. At the same time there will be joy, peace, and blessing. Greatest of all, Christ will be with us to care for us and provide all our needs every step of the way. He will never leave us nor forsake us.

This journey can either be a thrilling experience or dull and uninteresting. Actually, to a large degree it will depend on what we make it. We have a choice of victory or defeat.

What you will read in the following pages will offer positive suggestions for victory in your new life. Take them to heart, and do your best to follow through in the strength of the Lord.

Chapter 1

BELIEVE AND KNOW IT

Jesus chose seventy disciples, endowed them with power to perform miracles, and sent them to serve Him. They returned, elated over the tremendous success, and declared, "Even devils were subject to us."

But the Lord shifted the trend of their conversation. "Notwithstanding in this rejoice not, that the spirits are subject unto you; but rather rejoice, because your names are written in heaven" (Luke 10:20). It would be wonderful to be able to perform miracles, but Christ emphasized a more important matter—to have our names written in the Lamb's Book of Life, to know we are ready to meet God. The Bible explains clearly the way of salvation God has provided. It tells us that receiving by faith Christ as Savior and Lord we can rejoice in knowing our sins are forgiven and our names are among the redeemed.

Paul had this remarkable experience on the road to Damascus. He renounced all efforts to save himself and recognized Christ as the way to eternal life. He had been a religious man, a "Hebrew of

Hebrews" of the tribe of Benjamin, a Pharisee. He had left no stone unturned in seeking to obtain salvation by his own efforts. He tithed without omitting the weightier matters of the law. He could have said with the young man who came to Jesus, "All these things have I kept from my youth" (Matt. 19:20). And so strongly did he think his way was right, he persecuted the Christians. But suddenly on the Damascus road Paul came to realize he was heading in the wrong direction, and what had seemed to be necessary had become worthless.

He relied totally on the merits of Christ.

Have you, like Paul, received Christ? If not, why are you waiting? Perhaps you are waiting for a vision or a voice. If so, you may never get saved. In His Word, the Bible, God has asked us to come to Him through faith in His Son Jesus Christ.

Turn to the living Christ, and ask Him to come into your life and to save you.

People who come to Christ sometimes later are not sure whether they are saved—they lack the assurance the true child of God should possess. If you are unsure of your salvation, here are some tests for self-examination. They all come from the first epistle of John, although other passages say much the same thing.

"If we love one another, God dwelleth in us, and his love is perfected in us" (1 John 4:12). "We know that we have passed from death unto life, because we love the brethren. He that loveth not his brother abideth in death" (1 John 3:14). Do you love the people of God, cherish fellowship with them, and are willing to help them when they are in need? Jesus said, "Inasmuch as ye have done it unto one of the least of these my brethren, ye have done it unto me" (Matt. 25:40).

Another test is found in 1 John 4:13, "Hereby know we that we dwell in him, and he in us, because he hath given us of his Spirit." The very moment one calls on Christ for salvation, he or she receives the Spirit of God. The Christian is "born of the Spirit" as we are told in John 3:5.

Is the Spirit of God living in you? This is not emotionalism or religious feeling but someone influencing you for good. If you are not aware of the Holy Spirit's presence, it is probable that He does not live with you. In Romans 8:8–9 we read, "So then they that are in the flesh cannot please God. But ye are not in the flesh, but in the Spirit, if so be that the Spirit of God dwell in you. Now if any man have not the Spirit of Christ, he is none of his."

One may be going through depression as the result of some sorrow and yet be aware of the inner peace the Holy Spirit gives. The apostle Paul wrote, "We are troubled on every side, yet not distressed; we are perplexed, but not in despair; Persecuted, but not forsaken; cast down, but not destroyed; Always bearing about in the body the dying of the Lord Jesus, that the life also of Jesus might be made manifest in our body" (2 Cor. 4:8–10).

The Apostle faced distress and yet was able to move on an even keel because of the presence of the Holy Spirit. If you do not know the Holy Spirit dwells within you, perhaps you have had only an emotional stirring instead of a real step of faith.

Another test of salvation is in 1 John 4:15. "Whosoever shall confess that Jesus is the Son of God, God dwelleth in him, and he in God." Christians declare their belief in Jesus Christ to those around them. Are you ashamed of the One who gave His life on the cross for you? Or do you speak boldly when God gives you the opportunity to let other people know you belong to Christ? "Whosoever therefore shall confess me before men," said Jesus, "him will I confess also before my Father which is in heaven. But whosoever shall deny me before men, him will I also deny before my Father which is in heaven" (Matt. 10:32–33).

To deny Christ, one needs only to remain silent when he or she has the opportunity to witness. One who has met the Lord will be anxious to help others come to know Him too. The believer will speak for Christ.

Another test in this epistle can give assurance. "And he that keepeth his commandments dwelleth in him, and he in him" (1 John 3:24). Obedience to God is a blessed sign of one who is in God's family. I'm not referring to the Ten Commandments alone for God has given in both the Old and New Testaments other commandments which are to be obeyed. The unsaved cannot obey them for they do not have the Spirit of God to give them power to obey. Only the one who has come to God through Christ has this power at his or her disposal.

Many people have a great deal of religious talk but little convincing action. They have outward piety, but are not changed within. Jesus said, "If ye love me, keep my commandments" (John 14:15). And again, "Ye are my friends, if ye do whatsoever I command you" (John 15:14). People can talk about God but unless they back it up with action, others have reason to doubt that they ever met the Lord. Those who love Christ will obey Him and seek to do His will as revealed in the Bible.

The question then arises, "Can a saved person be lost again?" A person who has entered into a personal relationship with Jesus Christ and measures up to the tests of a Christian in John's epistle may still lack assurance that he or she will "stay saved."

The Bible says, "For by grace are ye saved through faith; and that not of yourselves: it is the gift of God: Not of works, lest any man should boast" (Eph. 2:8–9). Salvation then is by God's grace and not by our works. That God has done this should assure us that it can't be undone. To believe otherwise detracts from His perfect work for us. Also, the fact that Jesus speaks about salvation as a new birth (John 3:3, 7) gives assurance that it is irreversible. As in physical birth, it is impossible to be "unborn." "But as many as received him, to them gave he the power to become the sons of God, even to them that believe on his name: Which were born, not of blood, nor of the will of the flesh, nor of the will of man, but of God" (John 1:12–13). The new birth is from God.

Further, the Bible assures us that when one believes, he or she receives *eternal* life—not temporary life. In John 3:16 we read, "For God so loved the world, that he gave his only begotten Son, that whosoever believeth in him should not perish, but have *everlasting* life." One cannot get the idea of "temporary" from the word "everlasting." That which is eternal never ends. Endless, continuous life is given by God to the one who places his or her trust in Christ.

Nowhere in the Bible are we told that anyone goes to heaven on the grounds of what he or she does. Heaven is granted only to those who have acknowledged that Jesus Christ died for their sins and rose from the grave in victory over death. If we could get to heaven on our own merit, Christ's sacrifice would have been unnecessary. Therefore, even if a saved person dies in a backslidden condition, he or she enters heaven for it has been purchased for that person by Christ. The backslidden Christian gains heaven, as it were, by the skin of one's teeth.

The believer is constantly urged in Scripture to not backslide but, if he or she does, to quickly return to God's fellowship.

In the explanation of the Communion Service in 1 Corinthians 11, Paul points out the importance of examining one's own heart before partaking of the elements. In Corinth some believers were coming to the Lord's table in an unworthy manner. They were backslidden in that they knew they had sin in their lives and were not willing to confess it. Paul referred to them as "weak and sickly." He further indicated that some had even died, as he used the term, "and many sleep." God judged them physically but this is not synonymous with spiritual judgment. They took sick and died and their bodies went to dust, but their souls went to heaven.

There is no reason for a Christian to be backslidden except by choice. "If we confess our sins," says the Word of God, "he is faithful and just to forgive us our sins, and to cleanse us from all unrighteousness" (1 John 1:9).

Some people wonder about Judas. He followed Christ for three years and did not go to heaven. Jesus said, "While I was with them in the world, I kept them in thy name: those that thou gavest me I have kept, and none of them is lost, but the son of perdition; that the scripture might be fulfilled" (John 17:12). In the upper room Jesus dipped bread into the cup of wine and gave it to Judas, the one who would betray Him. Scripture records, "After the sop Satan entered into him" (John 13:27). Judas received a demon, and no one possessed by a demon can go to heaven. Judas is not characteristic of the Christian. He was a pretender—not a backslider. A thin line is drawn between a backslider and a person such as Judas. Only God can tell the difference.

The important thing is to be sure we have repented of sin, acknowledged Christ's death on our behalf, and asked Him to come into our life. Then, if we follow the Lord daily in the power of the Holy Spirit, we will not doubt our salvation.

The Bible says, "He that endureth to the end shall be saved." This means we prove our salvation daily with holy living until we meet the Lord.

We have blessed assurance that not only do we belong to God now, but that we will be with the Lord when we die.

CHRIST KNOWS ME

I know not how the world turns 'round
   Nor how designs are formed in snow.
I do not know how stars stay up
   Nor how from seed the flowers grow.
I know not how 'lectricity speaks
   In instant voice o'er miles of space,
Nor how each element of earth
   Retains its weight and finds its place,
I know not how my heart responds
   To outside calls of joy or strife,
Nor how in turn my mind reacts
   To all the driving needs of life.
But I know Him who died for me,
   Yes, I know Him who set me free.
And one day sure, He'll come for me.
   Oh joy of joys, that Christ knows me!
                —Ed Steidman

Chapter 2

READ AND APPLY THE BIBLE

A survey of a thousand pastors, Sunday school teachers, and workers revealed that only fifty of them had read the Bible through, and of those who had read the Bible in its entirety only one out of ten had done so in a single year. Perhaps this explains why the church is impotent in these days of tremendous need.

Most of us read and study the Bible too slowly—by chapters or verses here and there rather than studying it as a book. We need to get an overview of the Bible to know and understand all of God's truth.

There is no book in all the world as profound and mighty as the Word of God. In Hebrews 4:12 we read that the "word of God is quick, and powerful, and sharper than any two-edged sword, piercing even to the dividing asunder of soul and spirit, and of the joints and marrow, and is a discerner of the thoughts and intents of the heart." Here is a book that can pierce the very conscience of man; a book that reveals the sinfulness of man, gives the only remedy for sin and evil, and points us to the way of everlasting life. This is the Word of the Lord.

In 2 Timothy 3:16–17 we are told "All scripture is given by inspiration of God, and is profitable for doctrine, for reproof, for correction, for instruction in righteousness: That the man of God may be perfect, throughly furnished unto all good works." God tells us all Scripture came from Him. In other words, all that was recorded in the original manuscripts is from God. For this reason, the Bible can rightfully be called the Word of God. The Bible is the only written revelation God has given of Himself, His purposes, and His plans.

The predominant theme throughout the Bible is God's plan for redeeming sinful man through His Son Jesus Christ. In the Old Testament God's program through Christ is foretold, and the New Testament records the fulfillment. The Bible does tell about creation and about the sun and the moon and the stars. But as someone has said, "The Bible is not written to teach us how the Heavens go, but how to go to Heaven." It is the story of the Son of God coming into the world to save us from our sins—how He was crucified, buried, resurrected, and ascended and how He will come again.

We are further told that "*all scripture* is profitable for doctrine." Notice that God says, "*all scripture* is profitable" and all scripture is inspired. There are some who like to take parts of the Bible and say, "This is God's Word," and exclude other parts. Either we must accept all as the Word of God or none of it. Our Lord assures us that it is all His Word, and it is all profitable. This is why every believer ought to read the entire Bible through time and time again. Some of us have selected portions we read repeatedly, but I think God wants us to read the entire Bible systematically. By reading three chapters a day and five chapters on Sunday the Bible can be read through once a year. I have sought to do this every year, and it has been a blessing to me.

We also read that "all scripture is profitable for reproof."

Even God's people are proud and arrogant at heart. But as we study the Bible, we see ourselves as we really are. We are convicted of our sin and our shortcomings. We need the daily reproval and rebuke of God's Truth. Without the Bible we have no conception of sin or what sin does to us. His Word brings us to our knees in humble penitence and confession to God. It is for this reason that many people have no time for the Bible. Since it makes them uncomfortable, they choose to ignore it altogether.

Not only is Scripture profitable for doctrine and reproof, but we also read that "all scripture is profitable for correction." God not only tells us what is wrong with us, He tells us what we can do about it. The Bible is the only book in the world that gives us the mind of God concerning right and wrong. There are many so-called authorities on every hand. One condemns a practice. Another says it is right. How are we to know which is right? God has not left us in the dark. In Isaiah 30:21 we read, "And thine ears shall hear a word behind thee, saying, This is the way, walk ye in it, when ye turn to the right hand, and when ye turn to the left." The Lord will lead us and direct us if we want to be led.

God also says that "all scripture is profitable for instruction in righteousness." How we need this instruction in our day. There are so many temptations on every side. We need a Book which will purify our hearts and cleanse our minds. In John 15:3 we read, "Now ye are clean through the word which I have spoken unto you." Our minds are soon tainted by the things we see and hear. We need the refreshing, cleansing power of God's Word.

Finally, these verses tell us that all Scripture is given "that the man of God may be perfect, throughly furnished unto all good works." The believer needs to mature into the fullness of the image of Christ. Many who believe on Christ don't grow spiritually. One reason for this is that they neglect the Word of God. In 1 Peter 2:2 we read, "As newborn babes, desire the sincere milk of the word, that ye may grow thereby." If you want to grow and be strong in the Lord, a few hasty minutes of reading and studying the Bible are not enough.

I believe everyone who is truly born again ought to have a time first thing in the morning to get alone with God's Word and to feed on the truth of the Scriptures. Most of us take time to eat breakfast even though it may be only a cup of coffee and a piece of toast. But often we let our souls starve. Some day your body will die and return to dust, but your soul will live for eternity. The best preparation you can make for that day is to get some soul nourishment from the Bread of Life—God's Word. But we also need this nourishment to live as spiritual Christians now.

Jesus said on one occasion, "Ye do err, not knowing the scriptures" (Matt. 22:29). How many mistakes we make simply because we do not take time to read the Scriptures. And how can we apply the Scriptures when we don't know them?

Christians who go from week to week without any kind of Bible reading and meditation are usually spiritually weak. They have little testimony for God.

The president of a Christian college told of a senior who came in to see him. This young man was frustrated and defeated and realized that he had to get down to business. He was to be graduated soon—at least he hoped to be graduated—and going out into the world to take his place in society. He had wasted much of his time in college and on several occasions had been called in for discipline. He opened his heart to the college president and told of some of the things he had been doing which were contrary to Christian standards. In other words he was out of fellowship with God. The college president let the young man talk himself out, and when he had nothing more to say, the president asked one question: "When did you last read your Bible?" With chagrin and embarrassment the young man replied, "I haven't read my Bible for a year." This was obvious, for one does not usually get into such a state when he or she stays close to the Word of God.

Maybe at this moment you are mixed up. You are convinced that you are saved. You have made a profession of faith, but you aren't growing as a Christian. When did you last read your Bible? Are you taking time each day to let God speak to you? There are no shortcuts.

Maybe you are a defeated Christian. You are bogged down with worries, distress, and sorrow. Perhaps it is because you are trying to face life in your own energy, which is nothing more than weakness. May I suggest that tomorrow morning you set the alarm a little earlier? Take time to meet God. Read His Word.

Take time even though you may have only a little time. Give God the opportunity to speak to you. This is important in Bible study. A great mathematician once said that if he were given only two minutes to solve a problem, he would spend one of those minutes in deciding the method by which he could reach the solution. This is excellent advice. Never be pressed or hurried when you read the Word of God.

In Psalm 46:10 we read, "Be still, and know that I am God." God speaks to us in the Scriptures. We must center our thoughts on Him and what He says to us. When we open the Book, we must recognize who it is that speaks—God the Maker of heaven and earth, God the Father of our Lord Jesus Christ, the God who shall judge the living and the dead.

Do you realize that after the earth is purified by fire (and that will come at the end of the Millennium) in preparation for the people of God, the only thing that will stand that fire will be the Word of God? We are told this in both the Old and the

New Testaments. In Isaiah 40:8 we read, "The grass withereth, the flower fadeth: but the word of our God shall stand for ever." Then in Matthew 24:35 we read, "Heaven and earth shall pass away, but my words shall not pass away." If God has given us a Book that will stand throughout eternity, shouldn't we who are in Christ be familiar with its contents?

Possibly you do not know the Author of this Book. You have not trusted Christ for salvation. The Bible says to you, "Whosoever shall call upon the name of the Lord shall be saved." Respond to this glorious truth. Call on Christ—the Living Word. Claim the blessings of salvation in Him. And then, daily go to the written Word and read of Him, and you will grow spiritually as you follow Him and do His will.

Thank God for His Word: "Heaven and earth shall pass away, but my words shall not pass away."

Chapter 3

TALK WITH GOD

Among the gracious invitations to followers of Christ is the one to "come boldly unto the throne of grace, that we may obtain mercy and find grace to help in time of need" (Heb. 4:16). This assures us we can be confident that He who invites us to pray will also answer us.

There are believers who think that God does not always answer prayer. The Lord answers all prayers of those who are in fellowship with Him. To be "in fellowship" means that one believes in Christ as Lord and daily seeks to live in His will. If there is unconfessed sin, prayer is in vain.

David said in Psalm 66:18, "If I regard iniquity in my heart, the Lord will not hear me." If you are a Christian living in sin which you are not willing to forsake for Christ, your praying is ineffectual until you get right with God. If we confess our sins to the Lord daily, and "walk in the light as He is in the light," then we may claim the promise our Lord gave us in John 15:7, "If ye abide in me, and my words abide in you, ye shall ask what ye will, and it shall be done unto you." Notice, God says,

"It shall be done." He will answer, but it may not be as we think He should. He will answer in a way that is for His glory.

There are three answers to prayer—Yes! No! Wait!—and the answer may depend on how we pray. True prayer is not an effort to enlist the will of God on the side of our desires, but rather to bring our desires into conformity with His will. This is necessary because of the tendency to be selfish in our prayers. God says in James 4:3, "Ye ask, and receive not, because ye ask amiss, that ye may consume it upon your lusts." As a result, God finds it necessary to answer our prayers by doing a work in our hearts, rather than by giving us that for which we prayed. He molds our desires to harmonize with His divine plan. Actually, the more we grow in God's grace, the more our praying will become Christ-centered rather than self-centered.

In James 5:16 we read that "the effectual fervent prayer of a righteous man availeth much." "Effectual" praying is Christ-centered praying. It grows out of complete surrender of our wills to the holy and perfect will of God. Our Lord Jesus Christ exemplified this principle so completely in the garden of Gethsemane. In spite of all that He had endured and all that was ahead of Him, He could pray, "Nevertheless, not my will but thine be done." No matter how important or needful our requests may seem to us, if they are not in accord with the will of God, they are not best for us.

If our hearts are clean and our motives in prayer are Christ-centered, we shall experience the mighty power of God and the reality of Matthew 21:22, "And all things, whatsoever ye shall ask in prayer, believing, ye shall receive." So often it is true as we read in James 4:2, "Ye have not, because ye ask not." Even though we may be in a position to pray effectively, if we neglect prayer, the results will be few.

Throughout the centuries, the people of God have taken

God at His Word and experienced the mighty miracles of faith. He says in Jeremiah 33:3, "Call unto me, and I will answer thee, and show thee great and mighty things, which thou knowest not." God's servants in every generation have seen these "great and mighty things" because of faithful and fervent prayer.

John Knox cried out to his heavenly Father with sincerity of heart, "Give me Scotland or I die." The Reformation was ushered in through the prayers of Martin Luther. The English revival under John Wesley was preceded by the prayers of saints. The Great Awakening in Scotland under John Livingston was heralded by an all-night prayer meeting in which five hundred souls were saved. When saints of God are serious about prayer, the results can be endless. But actually, how many believers are really praying as they should? We often hurry through a brief, perfunctory series of stereotyped and repetitious phrases and words that mean little to God and less to us. The "hit and run" type of praying accomplishes little. How few Christians even spend three minutes a day in prayer.

Yet God says, "Men ought always to pray and not to faint." "Watch and pray that ye enter not into temptation." "Pray without ceasing." "Praying always with all prayer and supplication in the Spirit." "In everything, by prayer and supplication . . . let your requests be made known unto God." Repeatedly throughout the Scriptures we find the call to prayer. Why some Christians do not pray is difficult to understand.

God still speaks to those who take the time to talk to Him. But we must take time. We are living in a day when everything is speeded up, but God cannot be pushed or rushed. We must do as He says in Psalm 27:14, "wait on the Lord."

So often we pray and feel that we must have the answer immediately. If God does not act instantly, we become discouraged and give up.

Few believers take full advantage of the power of prayer. Many of us are bogged down by care, worry, and fear. We find ourselves in this unhappy state because we do not take our burdens to the Lord. God never intended our minds to be so filled with stress and anxiety. He wants us to talk freely with Him as you would to your closest friend. He is the friend that sticks closer than a brother. Unload your cares and burdens on Him. Intercede for your loved ones and friends.

We must not, however, engage in foolish praying. That is, we should not ask God to do for us what we ought to do ourselves. Sometimes people pray, "Lord, draw me closer to Thyself." This should be the concern of every believer, but we can be guilty of merely praying this request while we do nothing about it. Whose responsibility is it, for those of us who know Christ, to get closer to Him? Is it God's or ours? The Lord has made every provision that you and I walk closely with Him. In fact, He says in James 4:8, "Draw nigh to God, and he will draw nigh to you." According to this verse, we are charged with the first move. It is foolish to pray for the Lord to draw us nearer to Himself unless we are willing to respond to the Spiritual exercises in His Word.

Another disturbing petition is "Lord, make me a better witness for Thee." Many who pray that the Lord will make them a better witness never speak to a lost soul. The responsibility to speak to the lost belongs to the believer. The Holy Spirit must work through us, but let us not ask God to do what we are expected to do.

Another foolish request is, "Lord, supply my every need." This intimates that we are expecting God to do something supernatural without our cooperation. Some who make this request are careless about their spending. Others ignore their stewardship responsibilities to God. I believe it would be possible in many instances for us to answer this prayer ourselves by being downright practical in the use of the money the Lord has entrusted to us. Our prayers, then, however well-meaning, will be useless unless we do our part.

Have you ever thought, if God is all-knowing, if He understands my situation, and if He has power to supply, why can't I pray once and let it go at that? Why do I have to go to God day after day with the same petition? I think I now have a better understanding of the value of importunity, as Christ taught it. Jesus says, "Ask, and it shall be given you; seek, and ye shall find; knock, and it shall be opened unto you." Each of these verbs is in the present tense, implying a continued action. In other words, God is saying keep on asking, "and it shall be given you." Keep on seeking, "and ye shall find." Keep on knocking, "and it shall be opened unto you." There is a strong indication that persistence in prayer opens the door to the blessing of God. The problem I had with importunity was that I thought that it meant repetition, and Christ condemns "vain repetition" (Matt. 6:7). But repetition and importunity are not synonymous. When Christ speaks about importunity in prayer, He is referring to a petition that is repeated because of its urgency. It is a matter of deep, heartfelt concern to the one who prays. Earnestness is involved, not wordiness. It is an anxious heart beseeching God for divine intervention.

We see importunity in the account of the Syrophoenician woman in Matthew 15. This woman came crying unto Jesus, "Have mercy on me, O Lord, thou son of David; my daughter is grievously vexed with a devil." What was our Lord's response? Silence. Even the disciples seemed more kind to this woman, for they urged Christ to do something that would satisfy her so she would leave. "She keeps crying after us," they said. Jesus replied, "I was sent only to the lost sheep of the house of Israel." But she continued to implore Him saying, "Lord, help me." Again he refused her, but she didn't give up, and Jesus answered, "O woman, great is thy faith: be it unto thee even as thou wilt." And we read that "her daughter was made whole from that very hour."

Here is an example of how the Lord responds to importunity in prayer. This woman continued to cry unto the Lord because she had a burdened heart. Hers was not vain repetition. She was concerned about her daughter. She believed Christ could help, and she refused to give up until He did. God rewarded her faith.

Are we concerned for the spiritually lost? If we want to witness effectively, we must also pray. We cannot expect to penetrate minds blinded by Satan except by prayer. It is through prayer that we overcome the devil and his work in the lives of men. Even in evangelistic meetings in our churches, this fact is often overlooked. Speaking time is far out of proportion to prayer time. Jesus declared in John 15:5, "Without me ye can do nothing." Also, if we are to be effectual witnesses, we must pray to be delivered from ourselves and recognize our dependence on Him in telling the Good News.

Christians should also pray for their country. The Lord has said, "If my people, which are called by my name, shall humble themselves, and pray, and seek my face, and turn from their wicked ways; then will I hear from heaven, and will forgive their sin, and will heal their land" (2 Chron. 7:14). We need to do everything we possibly can to counteract the evils of our day, and one way is to pray. National and world leaders need wisdom beyond themselves in this complex age, and we should show prayerful concern for them that they will look to the Lord for salvation and guidance.

We have emphasized the importance of prayer in the life of the Christian. The Bible tells us prayer to God must be made through the Lord Jesus Christ. He is the mediator. This means that if you do not personally know Him, you cannot approach God the Father. In John 14:6, Jesus says, "No man cometh unto the Father, but by me." If you have never received Christ into your life, ask Him to forgive your sins and to take over the direction of your life. Then you will have the privilege of prayer.

Chapter 4

WORSHIP GOD

Years ago a number of prominent literary men were assembled in a club room in London. They were discussing illustrious figures of the past when one suddenly asked, "Gentlemen, what would we do if Milton were to enter this room?" "Ah," replied one, "we would give him such an ovation as might compensate for the tardy recognition accorded him by the men of his day." "And if Shakespeare entered?" asked another. "We would arise and crown him master of song," was the answer. "And if Jesus Christ were to enter?" asked another. "I think," said Charles Lamb amid an intense silence, "we would all fall upon our faces."

The last answer suggested an attitude of worship for Jesus Christ. He *is* different. He was man and at the same time God. Christians often thank Him for salvation but do not give Him true worship, which includes appreciation of who He is. We thank God the Father for the grace and love He showed in sending His Son to redeem us yet forget to praise Him for who He is. We recognize the Holy Spirit as the third Person of the

Godhead, yet lack awareness that it is He who empowers us to worship.

The triune God is awesome. The fact that each member of the Godhead is an equal and distinct personality is reason enough to worship, but as we contemplate the many attributes of each, we become more humble and adoring. The English word "worship" means "worthship" denoting the worthiness of an individual to receive special honor in according with that worth.

Giving worship an all-encompassing definition is difficult. Many have tried. None is completely adequate. One has called it the "overflow of a grateful heart under a sense of divine favor." This definition carries the idea that worship is not something that has to be conjured up with great effort or under stress. It is something that springs naturally out of a full and grateful heart.

Another has suggested that worship is "the upspring of a heart that has known the Father as a giver, the Son as Savior, and Holy Spirit as the indwelling guest." This definition emphasized that only a true believer can worship the Father and Son through the power of the Holy Spirit.

Still another definition calls worship the "occupation of the heart, not with its needs or even with its blessings but with God Himself." This definition distinguishes between worship and praise or prayer. In prayer we are often concerned with our needs. Praise is often thanks to God for meeting our needs. But worship demands our attention to God Himself. Praise and prayer should be part of our worship, not a substitute.

One idea is obvious in all of these definitions: Worship is something we give to God. In the Bible we see examples of this kind of giving. One is the wise men coming to worship Jesus. A star was the divine guidance that brought them to the

Son of God. They came with gifts, and when they saw Him, they humbly fell down before Him in adoration.

Mary of Bethany also pictures the giving aspect of worship. The gift she brought to the Lord was very expensive, probably purchased at great sacrifice. She didn't keep some of it for herself, she brought it all to the Lord. Then in an act of devotion she anointed the Lord's feet, and putting aside all her pride, she dried His feet with her hair.

In l Corinthians 1:29 we read "That no flesh should glory in his presence." Our pride, talents, capabilities, however good from a human standpoint, have no place in our worship of God. As the star guided the wise men to the one they wished to worship, the Word of God is our guide to worship, and not only our guide, but our authority.

Worship figures prominently in both the Old and New Testaments. God has not given rules and regulations but rather broad principles to guide our worship. It is each Christian's responsibility to study the Scriptures with a desire to obey God's will in the matter of worship.

The Lord Jesus in talking to the woman at the well said, ". . . true worshipers shall worship the Father in spirit and in truth: for the Father seeketh such to worship him" (John 4:23). In these remarks the Lord Jesus Christ introduced changes in worship that came about with His advent.

Israel had worshiped Jehovah in awe and at a distance. The law had revealed only God's holiness and justice, but the Lord Jesus Christ revealed God's heart of love. He revealed God as Father, His Father and the Father of all who come into God's family by faith in Jesus Christ. Since only those who are in His family can call Him Father, only they can be true worshipers.

Jesus also said that we are to worship "in Spirit and in truth." Israel's worship had been as a nation. It had been characterized, to a large extent, by prescribed offerings. Christ's call was for individual, spiritual worship. In the Old Testament the Holy Spirit came upon certain ones for a specific purpose. The Lord Jesus announced that the Spirit would be within us. Since Pentecost all believers are indwelt by the Holy Spirit who empowers them to worship. The indwelling Spirit then is essential to worship.

Jesus in His talk with the woman at the well also said that worship was no longer to be confined to a certain place (John 4:21). The tabernacle and temple had been figures, they were replaced by Christ Himself.

However, worship is in no way limited to a place, to a day of the week, to a certain time. We who are redeemed can worship alone or in a group, in any place, any day, depending only on our spiritual condition. If we are in a state of spiritual poverty, we may have little within us to give. As we read God's Word and meditate on it, we will with the enabling of the Holy Spirit be able to give to God something of what He desires from our heart.

God has communicated His attributes to us in His Word. While we cannot understand all that is said about Him, a deeper appreciation is sure to result as we consider His holiness, His mercy, His grace, His glory.

It is also clear from Scripture that we are to worship Jesus Christ as well as the Father. In Philippians 2:9–10 we read, "Wherefore God also hath highly exalted him, and given him a name which is above every name: That at the name of Jesus every knee should bow, of things in heaven, and things in earth, and things under the earth."

We honor Him because He is the Son of God and the Son of man. He is the creator of all things, He is our Savior, He is our risen Lord, He is our intercessor. As we consider all He is, we too will say as did Thomas, "my Lord and my God" (John 20:28).

Thomas saw the Lord Jesus, the wise men saw Him, and we see Him by faith. The Bible tells us, "No man hath seen God at any time; the only begotten Son, which is in the bosom of the Father, he hath declared him" (John 1:18). We see the Father through the Son. In fact, Jesus said, "he that hath seen me hath seen the Father" (John 14:9). As we are occupied with the Lord Jesus, we will have a greater understanding of God's glory because He is described as being the "brightness of His glory."

Peter in his first epistle exhorts us to "offer up spiritual sacrifices, acceptable to God by Jesus Christ." God made us so we could communicate our worship in a variety of ways—in prayer and praise, in music, and in giving of our money. But some church services give little opportunity for real worship. They are highly structured, or they feature teaching and "taking in" which leaves little time for the "giving" of worship. Jesus instituted a remembrance service when He was on earth, the Lord's supper or what some call the Communion Service. "This do in remembrance of me," He told His disciples as He passed the bread as a symbol of His body and the cup as a symbol of His blood. "Worship is kindled on the fires of remembrance," said A. P. Gibbs.

Remembrance, then, is an important ingredient of worship, and worship is what God wants most from His children. There is no substitute. Anything that man worships in place of God is an idol. There is danger in worship services of becoming occupied with the place, the ceremony, or even the prayers or the words of men. Satan tries to hinder our worship in other ways too. Self will always try to interfere. Criticism and other bad attitudes hinder worship. For some worship just demands too much preparation, remembering, meditating, giving.

In Revelation we see a heavenly worship scene with the living creatures and elders singing, "Thou art worthy, O Lord, to receive glory and honor and power." This is a reminder that we will continue to worship in Heaven. In the meantime God has asked for our worship now.

These verses of W. B. Dick's hymn should be our expression:

> O God our Father, we would come to Thee
> In virtue of our Savior's precious blood;
> All distance gone; our souls by grace set free;
> We worship Thee, our Father and our God.
>
> We bow in worship now before Thy throne,
> By faith the Object of Thy love would see;
> Who, in the midst, His brethren's song doth lead.
> To Him, our Savior, shall the glory be!

Chapter 5

DESIRE GOD'S WILL

An old sailor tells how many years ago he was sailing in the desolate seas of Cape Horn looking for whales. One day while heading south in the face of a hard wind and making little headway, an idea suddenly came to him, "Why batter the ship against these waves? There are probably as many whales to the north as to the south. I'll run with the wind instead of against it." He changed the course of the ship and sailed north.

An hour later the lookout at the masthead shouted, "Boats ahead!" There were lifeboats with fourteen sailors, the only survivors of a ship that had burned ten days before. They had been praying for God to rescue them.

The old sailor said later, "I am a Christian. I begin each day with a prayer that God will use me to help someone, and I am convinced that God put into my mind the idea to change the course of my ship in order to save those fourteen lives."

We read in Acts chapter three how many years before, two disciples experienced a change in plans. The healing of the lame man was not on Peter and John's schedule the day they went up to the temple for a time of meditation. But it was on God's schedule. Nor did the lame man know that it was to be his red-letter day.

Living in the light of God's will is exciting. The unforeseen opportunity may bring greater blessing than what we had in mind. No wonder David prayed, "Teach me thy way, O Lord . . ." (Ps. 27:11).

When we desire God's will, He does lead us in the direction of greatest usefulness. Many Christians are of little help to others because they are following the way of the flesh. They are carnal and selfish and do not experience God's best. Jesus was the opposite. His life always exemplified the words of His prayer, ". . . nevertheless not my will, but thine, be done" (Luke 22:42). Christ's constant desire was to be God's obedient Son, to do the Father's will. Every child of God should have this desire. Someone has said, "To know the will of God is the greatest knowledge; to suffer the will of God, the greatest heroism; to do the will of God, the greatest achievement; to have the approval of God on your work, the greatest happiness."

Yet many Christians continue to direct their own lives. How much happier and satisfied they would be if they allowed God to take over. David prayed, "Cause me to hear thy lovingkindness in the morning; for in thee do I trust: cause me to know the way wherein I should walk; for I lift up my soul unto thee" (Ps. 143:8). And in the same Psalm, we read more of David's prayer, "Teach me to do thy will; for thou art my God." "Teach me to do thy will" should be our daily prayer.

God has a directive will and a permissive will. He created humans as free moral agents. One may be a Christian and yet be extremely selfish, living for self rather than living for the Lord.

There are also Christians who are more concerned about pleasing men than pleasing the Lord. No wonder there are so many unhappy Christians. The Lord said in John 13:17, "If ye know these things, happy are ye if ye do them." And, of course, if we do not obey God, we miss the supreme happiness He has for those who are His followers. God's Word is not only to be believed; it is to be obeyed. The blessing comes in obedience. Jesus said, "Ye are my friends, if ye do whatsoever I command you" (John 15:14).

It is possible to be trusting the Lord's love and care after a manner, to be occupied in His work, and to be giving generously to His cause and yet not be living pleasing to Him because of some disobedience to His will which is allowed to continue. Obedience is the sure way to a life of fuller blessing.

It matters little whether we are doing great or small things, whether or not we are appreciated by those whom we try to serve, whether we are prominent or obscure, whether we see much fruit or little. The paramount question is, "Am I in the place, the circumstances, the service, and condition of soul which pleases the Lord? Do I have His approval?" This is God's desire for us; that in all things, His purpose for our lives might have preeminence. This thought is expressed in Hebrews 13:20–21 where we read, "Now the God of peace, that brought again from the dead our Lord Jesus, that great shepherd of the sheep, through the blood of the everlasting covenant, Make you perfect in every good work to do his will, working in you that which is well-pleasing in his sight, through Jesus Christ; to whom be glory for ever and ever." The Lord wants to "make you perfect in every good work to do his will." He wants to work in you and do "that which is well-pleasing in his sight." You can make your own plans if you want. You can go your own way. The Lord will permit you to do this, but you will never find the joy and blessing intended for those who follow in the Lord's chosen paths.

Those who do their own planning sometimes bring misery on themselves. God's way is not guaranteed to be without pain, suffering, or sorrow. But even if He allows us to suffer affliction, there is a peace and brightness in it all, unknown to those who choose their own way. The Lord lightens the burden to suit the strength of the back, or He strengthens the back to bear the burden. The Christian desiring God's will can enter into each new day without fear, knowing that "The steps of a good man are ordered by the Lord: and he delighteth in his way" (Ps. 37:23). The good man is yielded to God. He knows God makes no mistakes and leads only in those paths that are for the believer's good.

If you want the Lord to be your guide, you must be willing to submit everything to His control. When it comes to submitting to the will of God, some of us are like the young man who completed college and then prayed, "Now, Lord, I want to give you my life for full-time Christian service. I am willing to go any place you want me to go. But if it's all the same with you, please let me serve you in California, where the weather is nice." There must be no stipulations on our part. If we desire God's will with the intention of obeying, He will reveal it to us. Wanting it, praying about it is not enough either. Many believers never know the will of God for their lives, because they do not really want to do God's will. If we are willing to resign our wills to God's, He will guide us. In the Bible He has given us many examples of persons who walked in God's will: Moses at the Red Sea, Joshua at the Jordan, Ruth in Bethlehem, David in the wilderness, Nehemiah in the court of the king, Jeremiah in prison, Peter on the housetop, Paul on the storm-tossed ship. All of these believers cried unto their unerring Guide who led them in the right way. The privilege they enjoyed is for us to enjoy.

Possibly you are not sure how you may know God's will for your life. There are several ways. First, God guides by His Word. There must be an unqualified acceptance of the authority of the Holy Scriptures as the Word of God. Where the Scriptures are explicit on a matter, nothing more is needed. If we hold back, we are disobeying rather than lacking guidance. The words of Abraham's servant illustrate guidance and obedience. "I being in the way, the Lord led me" (Gen. 24:27). He had definite instructions from his master. Obedience kept him in the way, and the Lord crowned the errand with success.

God also guides by His Holy Spirit. Romans 8:14 states, "For as many as are led by the Spirit of God, they are the sons of God."

F. B. Meyer said, "Whenever you are doubtful about your course, submit your judgment absolutely to the Spirit of God and ask Him to shut against you every door but the right one. Say, 'Blessed Spirit, I cast on Thee the entire responsibility of closing against my steps any and every course which is not of God. Let me hear Thy voice behind me whenever I turn to the right or the left.' . . . In the meanwhile, continue along the path which you have been already treading. It lies in front of you; pursue it. Abide in the calling in which you are called; keep on as you are unless you are clearly told to do something else. Expect to have as clear a door out as you had in, and if there is no indication to the contrary, consider the absence of indications. The Spirit of Jesus wants to be to you what He was to the apostle Paul and his companions in their journeys. Only be careful to obey His least prohibitions, and where after believing prayer there are no apparent hindrances, believe that you are on the way to everlasting blessing."

Another way God guides is by His providences. A closed door tells us to stand still; an open door may be God's way of telling us to move forward, but not if it means going against a

"Thus saith the Lord." A south wind is not the wind of God for you if it is taking you away from the will of God. Delays and hindrances do not prove that we are out of God's will. "The steps of a good man are ordered by the Lord," said the psalmist (37:23), and someone has suggested that the stops also are ordered by the Lord. Both are seen in one of Paul's experiences. Paul and Timothy "were forbidden of the Holy Ghost to preach the word in Asia" (Acts 16:6). When they got to Mysia, they tried to go northeast into Bithynia, "but the Spirit suffered them not." So they went down to the seaport of Troas. Paul had his vision of the Macedonian asking him to come over and help. So the next morning he and Timothy continued their journey westward and at last reached Philippi in Macedonia where the Lord blessed their ministry. They had two stops and a move.

If our plans run into a roadblock, we must take courage and watch and pray, and the Lord will guide us into His way. We must also recognize that the Lord guides us through spiritual leaders, such as pastors, Sunday school teachers, and other godly men and women.

Oftentimes, God speaks directly to one's conscience and gives the inner certainty of what to do. He speaks through Christian literature. But most important, our hearts must be constantly in tune with Him, that we can understand His will when He speaks.

Be assured that we shall not know His will simply by picking verses at random from the Bible. Nor is He likely to speak to us during a hasty five-minute prayer session in the morning or a sleepy sentence prayer before retiring. Nor will His plan be made known to us while we are indulging in questionable pastimes. We must put Him first in everything. And then, as we look into His Word and pray, He will guide us in the decisions of life. "If any of you lack wisdom, let him ask of

God, that giveth to all men liberally, and upbraideth not; and it shall be given him" (James 1:5).

Living in God's will is for believers in Christ. If you are not a believer, say yes to the gift of salvation He offers you through His Son Jesus Christ. Then tell Him you want His will for your life.

Chapter 6

WALK BY FAITH

Fear is one of the distinguishing characteristics of the present age. Fear of people, war, death, loss of health or money disturb our sleep and keep us from productive work. The Lord prophesied that men's hearts would fail them because of fear (Luke 21:26).

Since the day a frightened Adam hid in the garden, mankind has tried to escape this troublesome companion. But most attempts fail because we approach the problem from without rather than from within. Fears are not primarily products of our environment but of our troubled hearts.

Years ago the Chinese built the famous wall to protect them from barbaric hordes from the north. It was so high they knew no one could climb over it and so thick they thought nothing could break it down. They rejoiced in what appeared to be release from fear and sat back to enjoy their security. But during the first hundred years of the wall's existence, China was invaded three times. Not once did the barbaric hordes break down the wall or climb over the top. Each time they bribed the gatekeeper and marched right through the gates.

The tragic mistake the Chinese made is the same error that most of us make. We fail to recognize that fear must be dealt with inwardly as well as outwardly. In our anxious quest for security, we ignore this basic fact. We build our fortresses of fact and circumstances, confident that no ill can effect a breach. We work for money, confident we can weather any economic blizzard. We submit to periodic health checkups to help relieve the fear of death. We move from the crowded city to spacious suburbs to relax and "get away from it all." Yet after all this and more, we read the latest book on "How to Escape Fear." We are still restless and fearful.

Many depend on courage to counteract their fears. Courage is worthwhile. It may enable us to face and even temporarily conquer fear, but it cannot eradicate it. And in the quiet moments, fear will return.

God never intended that we be distressed and disturbed by harassing fears. "Fear thou not; for I am with thee," He tells us in Isaiah 41:10. What more do we need? "If God be for us, who can be against us?" (Rom. 8:31).

The first step in conquering fear is to be certain that God is for us. The Bible assures us that God is for those who love and honor His Son. In John 1:18 we read, "No man hath seen God at any time; the only begotten Son, which is in the bosom of the Father, he hath declared him." What we know about God, we learn through Jesus Christ, His Son. "Believe on the Lord Jesus Christ," the Bible says, "and thou shalt be saved" (Acts 16:31). Trusting Christ for salvation, then, is the initial step of faith. It is also the first step to conquering fear. After we have believed on Christ, we are to trust Him for everything. We are not to try to fight the battle of life in our own strength. In the face of bitter unrest, the prophet Nehemiah declared, "Our God shall fight for us" (Neh. 4:20). Faith is what prompted the prophet to say this. If you and I are to conquer the fears and anxieties of life that rob us of God-intended joy and equanimity, we must trust the Lord. Jesus said, "If thou canst believe, all things are possible to him that believeth" (Mark 9:23).

An authority in a large mental institution said, "If faith in God could be restored to our mental patients, 55 percent of them could go home in a few days."

Faith is the foundation of the Christian life. We were saved by faith. We walk by faith. We overcome the world by faith. Faith is not just an emotional quality, but an intellectual quality of belief and confidence. Faith is full trust in God. Faith is the inward witness and hope, the evidence of the unseen, the inner assurance that we possess through Christ. Faith is the believer's stronghold in which he or she prepares to step into the future. Faith is taking God at His Word and believing Him for all things.

Perhaps the Christian's worst sin is lack of faith. The chief of sins is unbelief. Israel was barred from the Promised Land forty years as the result of this sin. How frequently you and I have been kept from our promised lands and blessings because we have doubted God's ability or willingness or both. God asks us the same heart-searching question He asked ancient Israel, "How long will it be ere they believe me?" (Num. 14:11).

We may think that we have faith in God, but it is misplaced. We must examine our hearts constantly to be sure our faith is in the Lord Himself. People often say they have faith, but the question is, In what? In whom? Some have faith in other people, some in circumstances, while others may put faith in the fatalistic philosophy "What's to be, will be." The Bible says, "Have faith in God" (Mark 11:22). It is possible to think we have faith in God when we are actually relying on human resources.

We limit God when we neglect to claim the promises in the Bible. Often we don't look beyond our difficulties. We discuss our confusing problems with others and forget that it was God who asked, "Is anything too hard for the Lord?" (Gen. 18:14). Do we really believe He is a mighty God? Or is He helpless before the stern reality of sin, sickness, financial need, sorrow, and death? There is no room for doubt. We shall never know the resources of God until we attempt impossibilities with God. After His resurrection our Lord declared, "All power is given unto me in heaven and in earth" (Matt. 28:18). He who believes this truth will have no trouble expecting the miraculous. When we limit God in our minds, our hearts will lack faith.

Perhaps you feel there has been a lack of faith in your life. First, ask God for faith. The Bible tells us Jesus is "the author and finisher of our faith" (Heb. 12:2). This being true, we can go to Him every day and ask for a new supply of faith. The disciples recognized this need and said to the Lord, "Increase our faith" (Luke 17:5). Next, we can study God's Word. "Faith cometh by hearing, and hearing by the word of God" (Rom. 10:17). The Bible is full of promises that will strengthen our faith. The more we meditate upon God's Word, the more familiar it will become to us, and it will be easier to trust God. Understanding and knowing the promises of God, we will be in a position to plead the promises. God wants us to do this. David prayed, "Therefore now, Lord, let the thing that thou hast spoken concerning thy servant and concerning his house be established for ever, and do as thou hast said" (1 Chron. 17:23). "Do as thou hast said," David pleaded. He claimed the promises of God and trusted the Lord to undertake. This is the privilege of all believers. If we take God at His Word, we can expect great things, and we will witness His mighty hand at work.

For the believer in Christ, faith is essential for another reason. God has told us, "Without faith it is impossible to please him" (Heb. 11:6). Paul reminds us to "Walk by faith, not by sight" (2 Cor. 5:7). In the Old Testament we read, "The just shall live by his faith" (Hab. 2:4). Some tell us that after a man is forty, he ought not to think of switching jobs or doing anything daring. Abraham would never have fit in with this kind of thinking. He was seventy-five years old when God told him to leave Haran and to "get thee . . . unto a land that I will show thee" (Gen. 12:1). And we read, "So Abraham departed, as the Lord had spoken unto him" (v. 4). This is quite an old age for pioneering. As news of Abraham's leaving spread, imagine how the neighbors must have dropped by to tell him that he was foolish to leave for the unknown at his age. But Abraham had faith in God and obeyed him. Faith and obedience are inseparable. If we do not obey God, we do not really believe Him regardless of what we profess. The test of our faith is our obedience.

Abraham took his step of faith because he knew his Lord well. He knew that his great God would not fail him, and he was willing to go all the way. It isn't great faith that God expects so much as genuine faith. Jesus said, "If ye have faith as a grain of mustard seed, ye shall say unto this mountain, Remove hence to yonder place; and it shall remove; and nothing shall be impossible unto you" (Matt. 17:20). Genuine faith is dead to doubts, dumb to discouragements, blind to impossibilities and knows nothing but success. Faith is simply taking God at His Word. It is confidence in the Giver. We will expect God to work in our lives. If we expect Him to work, He will work. Someone has said that Columbus practically found America before he left Spain, and he was far from being surprised when he saw the Western continent. He would have been surprised if he had not seen it. This is the expectancy of faith. There is no room for doubt.

Late one night a Christian woman had occasion to go from New Jersey to New York by ferry. After leaving the ferry, she was approached by a man who asked, "Are you alone?" "No, sir," she replied. He dropped behind, but she still heard his footsteps as she walked through the deserted street. She asked God for protection. The steps quickened and again the man was at her side. "I thought you said you were not alone," he said. "I am not, sir," was her reply. There was a note of sarcasm in the man's voice as he said, "I don't see anyone. Who is with you?" "The Lord Jesus Christ and His angels," she replied. With the briefest possible pause, the man said, "You keep too good company for me," and he left in a hurry.

In Hebrews 13:5 we have the unchangeable promise of God, "I will never leave thee, nor forsake thee." We can know that whatever the circumstances, God is there. We read in Colossians 3:3, "your life is hid with Christ in God." We are surrounded by God. We are protected by God. For this reason we can say with David, "Our help is in the name of the Lord, who made heaven and earth" (Ps. 124:8). This is not to suggest that the road will always be easy. There are many things we cannot understand in life. But God understands them. He tells us in Isaiah 43:2, "When thou passest through the waters, I will be with thee; and through the rivers, they shall not overflow thee: when thou walkest through the fire, thou shalt not be burned; neither shall the flame kindle upon thee." We worry and fret, yet we have no reason to do so. Jesus said, "Oh thou of little faith, wherefore didst thou doubt?" (Matt. 14:31). Let's pray as the disciples did: Lord, increase our faith, help our unbelief.

Chapter 7

SHARE THE GOOD NEWS

God never does anything halfway. A deaf man with a speech impediment was brought to Christ. The Savior took him aside from the multitude and, touching his ears and mouth, said to him, "Be opened." And according to the record, "the string of his tongue was loosed, and he spake plain." Small wonder that the multitudes "were beyond measure astonished, saying, He hath done all things well: he maketh both the deaf to hear, and the dumb to speak" (Mark 7:35–37).

God's desire for us is that we be whole and complete. It is not enough to hear; He wants us to speak also. There are some people who revel in the Word of God. They study it. They analyze it. They delve deeply into its doctrines and its prophecies. They go to Bible conferences and listen to preaching and rejoice that they can feed upon God's Word. But there is one weakness. They hear, but they do not speak. They make no effort to pass on to others what they have learned. They simply take the truths of God for their own enjoyment and spiritual pleasure.

This is a selfish approach to the things of God, to merely take them for ourselves without regard for those around us who need to hear the Gospel. In Psalm 107:2 God says, "Let the redeemed of the Lord say so, whom he hath redeemed from the hand of the enemy." I am convinced that if all of the redeemed of the Lord were to really speak out for Christ, giving testimony here and there, the world could be reached for the Savior within this generation.

I think of one such witness, a New York policeman who performed his duties faithfully in one of the city's toughest neighborhoods not only with a strong arm but with spiritual power. The Bible was his handbook. It was not a rare sight to see him kneeling in prayer with teenage boys. "Most of these people need love and attention," he said. "They can be changed, but only the Gospel can change them. The Gospel of Christ can change anybody."

Many of us have forgotten that Jesus said, "Ye shall be witnesses unto me" (Acts 1:8). We were not saved merely to be happy. God set our feet on the solid rock and washed us from all our sins that we might tell others how they too can experience deliverance from sin.

The apostle Paul said, "I am not ashamed of the gospel of Christ: for it is the power of God unto salvation to every one that believeth; to the Jew first, and also to the Greek. For therein is the righteousness of God revealed from faith to faith: as it is written, The just shall live by faith" (Rom. 1:16–17).

We have a glorious Gospel, the Good News for the unsaved. It is a powerful message, but if we fail to communicate it to those who need it, how can they know?

A witness is not necessarily a preacher. He need not be eloquent. It's more important to have a heart overflowing with the love of God and a sincere concern for those who need to experience this love. Such a Christian will be well on the way to usefulness.

I recall reading, many years ago, of a man who commuted by train from his Long Island home to Manhattan. He was well dressed, affable, and kind. As his train left the station, he walked up and down the aisle speaking to the passengers. "Excuse me," he would say, "but if any of your family or any of your friends is blind, tell them to consult Dr. Garl. He restored my sight."

For many years this man had been totally blind, and it was Dr. Garl who performed an operation resulting in the restoration of his eyesight. The patient was ever grateful, and he wanted to get the word to all who were in the same plight. Courteously, courageously, confidently, he told of the great physical change that came into his life. God expects His followers to courteously, courageously, and confidently tell of the spiritual healing they have received from the Son of God.

Isn't it tragic that we who are in Christ know the One who can transform lives and we show so little concern. We remain silent. Why? Are we ashamed of Christ, or are we not satisfied with Him? There appear to be a variety of reasons—or excuses.

Some of us are too busy. We have too many involvements. We have driven our stakes too deep in the wrong places. We have overlooked the fact that we are pilgrims passing through this land; we are not permanent residents. We have not got hold of the fact that for the few short years we are here, there is a job for each of us to do.

Many are cold and indifferent when it comes to communicating the Gospel, living for self rather than for Christ. Some are fearful of what people might think or say. What does it matter? Is it not more important to consider what God thinks about us and how we are performing as Christ's representatives?

Clyde Taylor, a Christian statesman in Washington, was a man of vision and concern for the unsaved. After attending a reception of the State Department and watching the ambassadors from the different countries parade in, Dr. Taylor said, "You never find one of these ambassadors who is suffering from too much humility. But do you know what disturbs me? When I meet Christians who represent the Lord Jesus Christ, it is a military secret. Why should we ever be embarrassed to say, 'I am an ambassador for the Lord Jesus Christ'? In my job in Washington, D.C., that language is understood and appreciated and never looked down upon. I have never had any derogatory remarks made in Washington because of my testimony of faith in Jesus Christ. What are we afraid of? We are ambassadors for Christ. Examine the fifth chapter of 2 Corinthians. In verse 20 we read, 'Now then we are ambassadors for Christ, as though God did beseech you by us: we pray you in Christ's stead, be ye reconciled to God.'"

Others say, "I don't know enough about the Bible," but if they have been saved from sin and have new life in Jesus, they have a personal experience to share. Jesus said in Matthew 12:34, "Out of the abundance of the heart the mouth speaketh." Even those with seemingly severe limitations have a testimony for the Savior.

J. Oswald Sanders tells about visiting a Christian woman who had neither arms nor legs, just a pitiful stump of a body. She had not moved from her room in forty-three years. She was never free from pain. As Mr. Sanders entered her cottage, he noticed that she had named it "Glad Wish." When he came into her presence, it was not to see a depressed invalid but a radiant Christian. When the calamity had overtaken her, instead of rebelling against God, she took it from Him as a discipline. With rubber attachments and a pen she had learned to write and penned letters on copper foil. She started a correspondence which circled the globe. People began to visit her in her room seeking spiritual help. She showed Mr. Sanders letters from people all over the world whom she had led to Christ either in that room or through her correspondence. The circumstances which might have crushed or embittered her served only to sweeten and make her more like the Master she loved and served. How do we explain such love and devotion? Full commitment to God is the only answer.

Many who profess to be believers have little or no concern for the lost because their lives are not fully committed to Christ. I firmly believe the first step in becoming a soul winner is to surrender completely to the Lord. Our worst sin is selfishness. Christ said, "If any man will come after me, let him deny himself, and take up his cross, and follow me" (Matt. 16:24). The selfish Christian will never be a soul winner. He will always be occupied with something he considers more important. Self must be defeated, and Christ must have first place in everything.

A friend tells of his visit to a lighthouse. "Are you not afraid to live here?" he asked the keeper. "Not at all," was his reply. "We never think of ourselves." "Never think of yourselves! How is that?" asked the visitor. "We know that we are perfectly safe and only think of having our lamps burning brightly and keeping the reflectors clear, that those in danger may be saved."

We who are believers in Christ are safe in a house built on a rock which cannot be harmed by the wildest storms. In a spirit of love, devoid of selfishness, we should keep our light shining brightly for Christ that those all around, struggling in the sea of sin, might find forgiveness in Christ Jesus.

I heard of a pastor who was greatly disturbed over the fact

that his people were not witnessing for Christ. He preached sermon after sermon on this obligation, but there seemed to be few results. Then he decided to try a different approach, to start with the officers of his church. "How many of you men," he asked, "have ever led a lost soul to Jesus Christ?" There were fifteen present. Five were able to say they had experienced this joy. Ten were silent. One of the officers later confessed to the pastor that the question had so convicted him that the same night he went home and spoke to his three boys about Christ.

How tragic it is that Christians have such little concern for loved ones, friends, and neighbors who are without Christ. If you are a child of God, I wonder what your answer would be to this pastor's question. Because of someone's faithful witness, you came to Christ. Have you been doing your best to lead others to the Savior?

Have you ever considered Christ's example of concern? "And when He (the Lord Jesus) was come near, he beheld the city, and wept over it." The Lord Jesus was preparing to enter Jerusalem, but as he descended the Mount of Olives where He could overlook Jerusalem, He paused to reflect on the situation and began to cry. Our Lord wept because He saw men and women, boys and girls bound by religious tradition but without hope and without God. He knew all about the hardness of their hearts, and because of His great concern, He wept. Our Lord was burdened to see others reached for God.

An unbelieving lawyer once said, "If I believed the masses are perishing in sin, I could have no rest. I would fly to tell them of salvation. I would labor day and night. I would speak it with all the pathos I could summon. I would warn and entreat my fellow human beings to turn to Christ. I am astonished at the manner in which the majority of you Christians give forth your message. Why do you not act as if you believed your own words? You do not have the earnestness that we lawyers have in pleading. If we were as tame as you are, we would never carry a single suit."

Instead of being convincing witnesses, we substitute other efforts in the name of evangelism. We build lovely churches and casually wait for the people to come to hear our preacher. But this is not evangelism. Jesus declared in Matthew 13:38, "The field is the world." He also said the "seed" is to be sown in the "field." What would you think of a farmer who stood on his own doorstep and sowed it knee-deep in wheat? What kind of harvest would he reap? Instead of waiting for those outside of Christ to come to us for life, our Lord told us to "go into all the world and preach the Gospel." Are we taking our opportunities?

Ask God to lay on your heart one person, whether in your business, in your church, in your neighborhood, in your school. Just one, not a dozen, not everybody on the team or in your homeroom or in your office—just one person. Pray that God will give you the grace to befriend that one and stay with and work with that person until that person decides for Christ. Communicate, get involved, and the Spirit of the Lord will bless your efforts.

And don't overlook the opportunity to disseminate the message of life through Gospel literature. Such a ministry does not demand a college education or great skill, but merely a heart filled with the love of Christ and an alertness to opportunities for distributing a tract and saying a word.

A Christian in one of the southern states places tract racks in service stations around town. At regular intervals he returns to fill the racks. He is amazed how quickly the tracts are taken. This same man frequently distributes tracts door-to-door. In another town there is a shut-in who could easily excuse herself from Christian service because of her disability. But she has a heart overflowing with love for the lost. Daily she scans the newspapers for those who are in trouble or bereaved. Writing a brief personal note, she encloses a helpful tract and then prays that God will use this means to point the distressed soul to the One who alone gives peace.

In Indiana there is a druggist who encloses a tract with every package of medicine he delivers. He testifies that the blessing of God on this ministry has been unlimited. He has seen souls saved through this method of spreading the truth.

Some Christians enclose Gospel tracts when paying their monthly bills by mail. A consecrated machinist was concerned about giving the Gospel in print to those attending the County Fair. He succeeded in getting Christians to pray while he and a friend distributed nine thousand tracts among the Fair visitors.

Tracts must be used prayerfully. All witnessing needs prayer-backing. Nothing can be accomplished for God in any phase of His service without prayer. The work of saving and transforming the lives of humans is the task of the Holy Spirit. We do the planting, but the Spirit of God does the convicting.

Never expect that soul winning will be easy. For most of us, it is the most difficult work God asks us to do. The devil opposes it bitterly. He strikes hardest and most effectively at the forces which provide the greatest threat to his cause. The believer who commits fully to Christ and vows to be a faithful witness, at the same time summons the devil to a life-and-death conflict. To be sure, he will accept the challenge. He will discourage you, rebuke you, and embarrass you. If you don't keep your eyes fixed on Christ, you will soon give up.

God has told us in His Word that He wants everyone to be saved and to come unto the knowledge of the truth. Our God is concerned about the salvation of every man, woman, boy, and girl on earth. Are we?

Have you been a silent Christian? Some people seem to be a Christian only when they go into the house of God. No one would know they belong to Him during the rest of the time because they never speak for Him.

Perhaps you have never spoken for Him and about Him because you don't really know Him. Ask Christ to come into your life, commit all to Him, and then share your experience with others.

Chapter 8

LOVE EVERYONE

Love should be the distinguishing characteristic of those who are reborn by the Spirit of God. Jesus said, "By this shall all men know that ye are my disciples, if ye have love one to another" (John 13:35).

The early church astounded the pagan world with its demonstration of love in the lives of believers, but the church today is marked with strife and division. Paul wrote, ". . . walk worthy of the vocation wherewith ye are called, With all lowliness and meekness, with longsuffering, forbearing one another in love; Endeavoring to keep the unity of the Spirit in the bond of peace. There is one body, and one Spirit, even as ye are called in one hope of your calling; One Lord, one faith, one baptism, One God and Father of all, who is above all, and through all, and in you all" (Eph. 4:1–6). Unity and oneness are predominant truths in these verses. Both express the idea that those who profess to be followers of Jesus Christ should walk and work together in love. This is not mere emotional love but that which is a practical demonstration sometimes involving sacrifice or suffering.

In 1 Corinthians 13, the great Love Chapter, we read that "Charity suffereth long, and is kind; charity envieth not; charity vaunteth not itself, is not puffed up." The word "charity" here means "love." Those of us who have experienced the love of God should be kind. If you are a believer, do others know you because of the overflowing measure of Christ's love in your life? Or are you known for being critical, harsh, and unkind?

In Galatians 5:22 we read that "the fruit of the Spirit is love," and then from this fruit comes such graces as "joy, peace, longsuffering, gentleness, goodness, faith, meekness, temperance." Without love, however, these graces will be unknown, for "joy" is love exulting, "peace" is love in repose, "longsuffering" is love untiring, "gentleness" is love in doing, "goodness" is love in action, "faith" is love in trusting, "meekness" is love under discipline, "temperance" is love in training.

It is easy to love those who love us, to love the lovely, but Christ said we are to love the unlovely. We are to love those who hate us, and love that is real and sincere must be demonstrated. It must be proved.

It is difficult always to practice this love. It takes much grace to be patient with people who are selfish, thoughtless, discourteous, ungrateful, and censorious. But our Lord said, "Love your enemies, bless them that curse you, do good to them that hate you, and pray for them which despitefully use you, and persecute you" (Matt. 5:44). He also said, "Vengeance is mine." We are not to fight back when offended. We are called to be peacemakers. "Blessed are the peacemakers: for they shall be called the children of God" (Matt. 5:9).

There is a great temptation to do only what we think is expected of us. Few of us even do that. But the Bible tells us repeatedly to go far beyond the line of duty. In His Sermon on the Mount Jesus said, "But I say unto you, That ye resist not evil: but whosoever shall smite thee on thy right cheek, turn to him the other also. And if any man will sue thee at the law, and take away thy coat, let him have thy cloak also. And whosoever shall compel thee to go a mile, go with him twain" (Matt. 5:39–41). Jesus not only taught these things, He did them! He tells you and me that the servant is no greater than his Lord. What Jesus did, we are supposed to do.

When you trust in Jesus Christ and become a partaker of the divine nature, your sin is forgiven and you are forever delivered from the condemnation that rested on you. But this is just the beginning of the Christian life. The believer is told to "grow in grace, and in the knowledge of our Lord and Savior Jesus Christ" (2 Peter 3:18). How do we grow? Peter tells us in the first chapter of his second epistle that certain things should be added to our lives along the way, ". . . add to your faith virtue; and to virtue knowledge; And to knowledge temperance; and to temperance patience; and to patience godliness; And to godliness brotherly kindness; and to brotherly kindness charity. For if these things be in you, and abound, they make you that ye shall neither be barren nor unfruitful in the knowledge of our Lord Jesus Christ." We read in the Bible how the disciples, as new creatures in Christ, grew into loving unselfish and zealous heralds of the Gospel of Christ.

If a baby does not grow, the parents are rightfully concerned. The same is true when one is born into the family of God by faith in Christ. There must be growth, and an evidence of growth is loving kindness toward others. It is a must in the believer's life if he is to be an effective Christian.

It is regrettable that many who claim to be in the light of the Lord do not follow Christ in a life of kindness and consideration for others. Jesus said, "Inasmuch as ye have done it unto one of the least of these my brethren, ye have done it unto me" (Matt. 25:40). Whatever we do for others we do for Christ.

Paul wrote, "Bear ye one another's burdens, and so fulfill the law of Christ" (Gal. 6:2), that is, the principle of Christ. The Lord Jesus practiced this principle of kindness wherever He went—to the woman taken in adultery, to the leper, to the sick woman who reached out and touched His garment. We see in the Gospels, time and time again, Christ's concern for other's needs. He is just as concerned today. Believers have the privilege of taking cares and sorrows to the Lord Jesus in prayer, with the assurance that He will hear and undertake. As our Lord manifests this care for His own, we are in turn to constantly show it to others. Paul tells us we are to "Rejoice with them that do rejoice, and weep with them that weep" (Rom. 12:15). God has commissioned us to be sympathetic to the needs of others. But sympathy involves more than words. Action must back up words. Onesiphorus provides an excellent example of this. Paul, in writing his letter to young Timothy, tells of this servant's help to him, "For he oft refreshed me, and was not ashamed of my chain . . . he sought me out very diligently, and found me . . . in . . . many things he ministered unto me" (2 Tim. 1:16–18).

Christianity is not a mere intellectual assent to doctrine, important as sound doctrine may be in these apostate times. It is doctrine in action. Christianity is not simply a state of being. It is the business of doing—doing good for others. No one ever became a Christian by doing good, but if one is a Christian, he ought to be doing good. Jesus said, "Let your light so shine before men, that they may see your good works, and glorify your Father which is in heaven" (Matt. 5:16).

It is so easy to live for oneself and completely overlook the needs of our neighbor. I cannot but feel that there are Christians who suffer nervous disorders simply because they have catered too much to self and not enough to others. They live within themselves. The world seems to revolve around their own interests. A good antidote for depression is to go out and do some thing for somebody else.

Among those we read about in the Bible who were faithful in their concern for others was Esther who risked her life by coming unbidden before the king in order that she might save her people. There was also Jonathan who unselfishly withdrew so that his friend David might ascend the throne that otherwise would have been his.

Florence Nightingale, with loving concern for suffering humanity, organized a corps of nurses in the face of severe criticism.

Someone has said, "You cannot get your mind off yourself unless you get it on others." God says, "Look not every man on his own things, but every man also on the things of others" (Phil. 2:4).

Is there someone you can help today? Have you called on that sick friend recently? Have you remembered him in some way to help encourage and cheer him in his time of affliction? What about that shut-in who hasn't seen the outside world for many months, possibly even years? Have you taken some of the joy from the outside to her, that her long hours might be shortened? What about that friend who is going through financial difficulty? Have you helped?

Another necessary part of Christian love is forgiveness. Jesus frequently talked about Christians and forgiveness. In His model prayer He said, "Forgive us our debts, as we forgive our debtors" (Matt. 6:12). Later in this same chapter we read, "For if ye forgive men their trespasses, your heavenly Father will also forgive you: But if ye forgive not men their trespasses, neither will your Father forgive your trespasses."

In Colossians 3:13–14, Paul says, "Forbearing one another, and forgiving one another, if any man have a quarrel against any: even as Christ forgave you, so also do ye. And above all these things put on charity, which is the bond of perfectness." Consider these words, "Even as Christ forgave you, so also do ye." Of course, forgiveness must be from the heart. Mere outward forgiveness, while nourishing a grudge, is not sufficient. "The Lord looketh on the heart" (1 Sam. 16:7). If a fellow Christian wrongs you, you are to go and discuss it with him or her. If the person repents, it is your duty to forgive. In many cases there is fault on both sides, and in such instances we are powerless to help others until our own guilt is confessed to God. Jesus said, "Judge not, that ye be not judged. For with what judgment ye judge, ye shall be judged: and with what measure ye mete, it shall be measured to you again. And why beholdest thou the mote that is in thy brother's eye, but considerest not the beam that is in thine own eye? Or how wilt thou say to thy brother, Let me pull out the mote out of thine eye; and, behold, a beam is in thine own eye? Thou hypocrite, first cast out the beam out of thine own eye; and then shalt thou see clearly to cast out the mote out of thy brother's eye" (Matt. 7:1–5).

If you have an unforgiving spirit, the presence of this disorder suggests that it is possible that you have never really been born again. You are a professor of Christ but not a possessor of Christ. Why not make sure of your salvation? Turn to the Son of God and ask Him to become your Savior and your Lord. If you do, He will give you the grace and love to forgive.

I don't know of anything that can hinder one's testimony of Christ more than an unforgiving spirit or a lack of kindness in one's life. So often we are guilty without even realizing it. It is so easy to talk ourselves out of some of our Christian obligations and to overlook the need to frequently confess.

Not only does one's spiritual health suffer from a lack of forgiveness, but his physical health as well. A New York physician reports that 70 percent of his patients reveal resentment in their case histories—resentment resulting from an unforgiving spirit. We cannot profess to be followers of the Lord while we harbor hatred in our heart toward others.

Christians should also be concerned about their treatment of believers who yield to temptation and fall into sin. One passage on the subject is Galatians 6:1–3, "Brethren, if a man be overtaken in a fault, ye which are spiritual, restore such an one in the spirit of meekness; considering thyself, lest thou also be tempted. Bear ye one another's burdens, and so fulfill the law of Christ. For if a man think himself to be something, when he is nothing, he deceiveth himself." "Brethren" suggests the unity of the Spirit that should prevail among believers. The word "fault" is really the word for "transgressions." The Bible says to "restore" the one who has yielded to sin. Don't criticize! Don't condemn!

It is said that when a sheep becomes sick, very often the others will turn on him and if possible will trample him until he is helpless. In His Word God frequently speaks of His people as sheep, and this is the way some Christians react when others become spiritually sick and fall into sin. Believers may worship together, pray together, and serve the Lord together, but if one falls short of what the rest think he or she should be, the entire group may turn on that one. They gossip or they condemn. They make that Christian feel like an outcast.

David was out of fellowship with God for an entire year after he had committed adultery and murder. One of the reasons he stayed away from the Lord rather than confessing may have been the attitude of his brethren. He wrote later, "I looked on my right hand, and beheld, but there was no man that would know me: refuge failed me; no man cared for my soul" (Ps. 142:4). The Lord Jesus is concerned about everyone, and you and I should be as well. He says if we claim to be "spiritual," then we are to "restore such an one in the spirit of meekness." "Meekness" is one of the fruits of the spirit, and the word suggests working with the one who is in need in the same manner in which a physician seeks to set a broken bone. The doctor does it with tenderness and kindness. This should be the believer's attitude as he or she seeks to help a fallen fellow Christian.

Jesus did not hesitate to mingle with publicans and sinners in order to help them, even though it was suggested to Him that He might become contaminated by close association with them. He crossed the barrier between Jew and Samaritan regardless of criticism because He wanted to spread the Good News. His great love for mankind led Him to the cross where He sacrificed Himself for the sake of others. As He hung on the cross, His enemies shouted, "He saved others; himself he cannot save." He was not interested in saving Himself. He did not come into the world for that purpose. Christ "came to seek and to save the lost." This was His mission. This should be the mission of every follower of Christ. We are not here to serve ourselves; we are here to serve Him.

Chapter 9

DENY SELF

"What is the chief problem of your ministry?" someone asked the leader of one of the sessions at a pastor's conference. "Myself" was his realistic reply. To be sure, this is most everyone's chief problem.

The world is rampant with the age-old sin of selfishness. We have wars with nations coveting territory of other nations. Men and women think only of their personal comforts while millions perish with hunger and cold. Selfishness is seen in buses, in trains, in planes, on the highways, and in hotels and restaurants where thoughtless men and women ignore the welfare or rights of others. It is seen in the spirits of some employers who withhold reasonable wages from their employees, and also in the spirit of some employees with their unreasonable clamor for wage increases producing strikes and untold inconvenience.

The psychologists tell us the trouble with most people is egocentricity, which simply means that a person is self-engrossed. The outcome can be neurosis and emotional breakdown.

Dealing with the self-life is a constant battle for Christians as well as the unsaved. The devil seems to exert even greater pressure when the child of God desires victory over the self-life.

Some years ago Dr. A. T. Pierson wrote about the futility of the self-life in believers. "Much of our spiritual life has a great deal of the leaven of self corrupting in it," he said. "We are seeking self-advantage and self-glory, only on a higher level and of a more refined sort. Nothing is so hard to kill as pride and selfishness. Man is like an onion—layer after layer, and each a layer of self in some form. Strip off self-righteousness, and you will come to self-trust; get beneath this, and you will meet self-seeking and self-pleasing; and even when you think these are abandoned, self-will betrays its presence, if this seems stripped off, you find self-defense, and last of all, self-glory. And when even this seems abandoned, the heart of the human "onion"—most offensive of all—is the selfish PRIDE that boasts at last of being truly humble."

The children of God have no right to live for themselves, for they are God's possession. We read in 1 Corinthians 6:19–20, "Know ye not that your body is the temple of the Holy Ghost which is in you, which ye have of God, and ye are not your own? For ye are bought with a price: therefore glorify God in your body, and in your spirit, which are God's." He has given us talents to use for Him, yet we often wantonly betray our trust. We are so often cowardly in witnessing for Christ because the self-life is dominant.

An enthusiastic reporter recorded the experiences of a young couple who, several years ago, fled from society to make their home on a barren piece of land on the Gulf of Mexico, 120 miles from their nearest neighbor. The reporter wrote about their "perfect life." I would say the life the reporter described is the ultimate of the selfish will. The perfect life starts with receiving Christ and then forsaking self to follow Him. Jesus said, "Verily, verily, I say unto you, Except a corn of wheat fall into the ground and die, it abideth alone: but if it die, it bringeth forth much fruit" (John 12:24). He describes the life that dies to self and becomes alive to Him. This is the life that sacrifices for God, that spends itself to do the will of God.

It was this spirit that constrained God to send His Son into the world rather than to dwell in isolated splendor, ignoring the heartbreaking needs of sinful humanity. And it was the unselfish nature of Christ that brought Him to die on the cross. Our Lord didn't think of Himself when He went to the cross. He thought only of lost humanity and our need for redemption. This is the Christ spirit.

Totally opposite is Satan's spirit. At one time, Satan was a beautiful angel, but he said in his heart, "I will ascend into heaven, I will exalt my throne above the stars of God: I will sit also upon the mount of the congregation, in the sides of the north: I will ascend above the heights of the clouds; I will be like the most High" (Isa. 14:13–14). Because of his selfish and rebellious spirit, he was cast from his high and noble position and became the instigator of evil. Millions of people in this world are mastered by this same selfishness. Everything they do is motivated by benefit to self. After one comes to Christ and is born again, it should be different. The true believer enters into Calvary's love. This kind of love "seeketh not her own" (1 Cor. 13:5). It never looks inward. It looks outward.

We shall never be effective for God until we are willing to deny self and let the Lord Jesus have the preeminence. He said in Matthew 16:24, "If any man will come after me, let him deny himself, and take up his cross, and follow me."

Jesus didn't mean that we should follow Him simply to be saved, but throughout life—hour by hour, moment by moment.

In a group prayer meeting an African Christian prayed, "Oh Lord, Thou art the needle and I am the cotton." That may seem like a strange prayer, but it was a vivid word picture of a Christian following Christ. The African had visited a mission school that day and, while watching the girls sew, had observed that the cotton thread always followed the needle. Christ wants those who believe in Him to be close to Him at all times, to be completely yielded to Him, to follow Him as directly and dependently as the thread follows the needle. The apostle Paul was able to say, "For me to live is Christ, and to die is gain" (Phil. 1:21). This is what it means to follow Christ. Regardless of what comes our way—sunshine or rain, joy or sorrow, peace or turmoil—to follow Him.

Many have to say, "For me to live is my business." To others it is pleasure, my family, or dozens of other interests that turn us from our supreme object in life.

Not long ago a man whose net worth was $50,000 said, "In about ten years I expect to be a millionaire." He had a goal and was extending his talent and energy to arrive at it as soon as possible. Ten years wasn't too long to wait to be as rich as he wanted to be.

A young medical student declares, "I'm going to be a heart specialist." She knows it means many years of schooling, but she determined to sacrifice to attain her goal.

If we do not establish goals, we live aimlessly—only for the present—doing what is exciting today without concern for tomorrow. Goals in the Christian life should be the outgrowth of the Christian's closeness to Jesus Christ. The Lord said, "Whosoever will save his life shall lose it: but whosoever will lose his life for my sake, the same shall save it" (Luke 9:24). Christ was talking about having a purpose in life outside of one's self, about having goals that terminate in eternity. He was talking about forgetting personal gain to serve others. The principle He taught is backward as far as many in the world are concerned. They say you lose by giving yourself to others. But once we've given our life to Christ, we are to live by divine principles.

The apostle Paul expressed his goal in life! To the church at Philippi he wrote, "That I may know him, and the power of his resurrection, and the fellowship of his sufferings, being made conformable unto his death; If by any means I might attain unto the resurrection of the dead . . . I press toward the mark for the prize of the high calling of God in Christ Jesus." It was not easy for Paul to achieve his goal; there was a price to pay. "But what things were gain to me, those I counted loss for Christ. Yea doubtless, and I count all things but loss for the excellency of the knowledge of Christ Jesus my Lord: for whom I have suffered the loss of all things, and do count them but dung, that I may win Christ, And be found in him, not having mine own righteousness, which is of the law, but that which is through the faith of Christ, the righteousness which is of God by faith" (Phil. 3:7–9). Everything had to go except that which exalted the Lord Jesus Christ, for anything that did not exalt Christ was a hindrance to Paul's quest for his goal.

James Hisky, discussing college students and the symptoms of moral decline on the campus, says, "At the heart of the students' problem is their lack of meaning for living." Many have neither "God nor goal." Millions, on and off the campus, have no purpose in life other than to get three square meals a day and to live fairly comfortably. Some Christians, too, are without vision and without concern; living for themselves, they show little love for Christ or others.

In Proverbs 29:18 we read, "Where there is no vision, the people perish." If you and I who profess to be followers of Christ do not fix our eyes upon Him and follow Him, millions who have never heard the Gospel will perish without it. Only those who love Christ and obey Him give sacrificially of their time and money. They are the ones who are supporting the missionary program and witnessing to their neighbors and friends.

If you are mastered by self, you have never entered into the joy of living. Truly happy people do what they can to help others. In helping them, they create life for themselves. The story is told about two men who were traveling in the mountains on a bitter cold snowy day. Both were so frozen that they despaired of arriving at their destination alive. About that time, they stumbled over a man half-buried in the snow and nearly dead from exposure. One of the men suggested that they carry the unfortunate man with them, but the other refused to help, insisting that they would have all they could do to save themselves. One went on his way while the other shouldered the unconscious man and, with great difficulty, struggled on with his heavy burden. Through his extra exertion, he began to warm up and felt better in spite of the severe cold. And the nearly frozen fellow hanging on his shoulders felt the warmth, and by the time they arrived at the village, he had recovered consciousness. Shortly before arriving, they found the man who had refused to help, fallen by the wayside and frozen to death. When we reach out of ourselves to help someone, we save ourselves.

We can help those around us, and we must help those around us; but we can do this best if we are what God intends us to be. We can only be this as we commit ourselves fully to His control, unreservedly yielding to His Lordship. He wants to be more than our Savior. He did not save us simply to take us to Heaven. His purpose far exceeds that.

Paul wrote, "Let this mind be in you, which was also in Christ Jesus: Who being in the form of God, thought it not robbery to be equal with God: But made himself of no reputation, and took upon him the form of a servant, and was made in the likeness of men: And being found in fashion as a man, he humbled himself, and became obedient unto death, even the death of the cross" (Phil. 2:5–8). He was emphasizing that the Son of God was equal with the Father in power and authority, yet He left Heaven to come to earth, not to be a great teacher, but to be a Savior. He took upon Himself a body and was born as a baby. He suffered the usual privations of life and was taken as a young man and crucified on a cross. The perfect, holy Son of God was humble. The apostle Paul pleads with us to be humble as Christ is. Humility is impossible as long as pride reigns in our lives. Pride is first on a list of things that God hates (Prov. 6:16–19). One may not have many worldly possessions, yet be extremely proud. One may not be handsome or attractive, yet be proud. The misleading thing about pride is that it is always obvious in the other person but we rarely detect it in ourselves. Someone has said, "The greatest of faults is to be conscious of none." Pride is at the root of many disturbances in the world. Pride gives no consideration to wisdom. Pride can never reason things out. Pride wants what it wants at any cost, and very often it will pay any price to get it. This is the thing God says He hates.

The mighty Nebuchadnezzar who is portrayed in the book of Daniel had a wonderful estimation of himself. He was extremely proud. He had a huge golden image of himself constructed and issued a decree that everyone should bow and worship this image. Later, this selfish monarch was humiliated. God made him as a beast of the fields, eating the grass of the field as the oxen. He was a living example of Proverbs 16:18, "Pride goeth before destruction, and an haughty spirit before a fall." The psalmist wrote, "Lift not up your horn on high: speak not with a stiff neck. For promotion cometh neither from the east, nor from the west, nor from the south. But

God is the judge: he putteth down one, and setteth up another"
(Ps. 75:5–7). These verses present a strong warning against
pride. The lifting up of the horn on high is really an attempt of
man to flaunt himself before God. Actually, this is what the
proud man does. He feels within himself a certain sense of
superiority that God has not intended for any man. It is important that we let the Lord have first place regardless of the
consequences. For the believer in Christ, this means a life of
humility. In practically every church there are factions and
divisions which are usually the result of personality conflicts.
Some people never seem to learn how to get along with each
other, and they refuse to give in. I have been told that if two
goats meet each other in a narrow path where they cannot turn
back and they cannot pass one another, they do not butt each
other and fight and try to knock the other out of the way. One
lies down so the other can pass over it. All of us could learn a
lesson from the goat.

In James we read, "God resisteth the proud, but giveth grace
unto the humble." This word "resist" means "to set one's self
against." God sets Himself against the proud. God exhorts the
believer saying, "Humble yourselves in the sight of the Lord,
and he shall lift you up." Promotion comes not from ourselves.
We don't have to push ourselves ahead by telling everybody
what we have done. God knows all about that. He tells us,
"Humble yourself in My sight, and I will lift you up."

If you want to tell people what God has done for you, that's
a different thing. This is what Paul did. He said in Galatians
6:14, "But God forbid that I should glory, save in the cross of
our Lord Jesus Christ, by whom the world is crucified unto
me, and I unto the world." Paul did some boasting, but not
about himself. About all he could say regarding himself was "I
know that in me (that is, in my flesh,) dwelleth no good thing"
(Rom. 7:18).

It is important that we look into our hearts to ask God to make us aware of our own pride. If you have thought you could get along without God, you are guilty of pride. You have gone through life the best you possibly could, ignoring the claims of Christ on your soul. God created us dependent beings. No one is self-sufficient. We need the help of the Lord in everything.

The stadium was packed, and the crowd had gathered to see the University of Southern California play its most important football game of the season. On the team was All-American Ed Smith. A few days before the game, the mother of this star player had died. She had followed her son's career with interest and delight. She was to have occupied a box seat at the game. Until game time it was not known by the crowd whether Ed would play or not. But when the team trotted on the field, there he was. A moment or two before the starting whistle, Ed walked over to the box where his mother would have sat. It was draped in black, and on the seat was a large picture of her. The big player stood before the picture a moment, and then as he turned to leave said, "Mother, I am playing this game for you." With that, he was off to add another brilliant performance to his record.

Such respect on the part of a son for his mother is certainly commendable. But if you are a Christian, think about the significance of this illustration. We who have truly believed on the Lord Jesus are God's own, and day by day, as we live before Him and as we desire to live for Him, He will give us the strength to do so.

Chapter 10

LIVE CONVINCINGLY

A certain minister seldom preached more than twenty minutes. When one of his faithful listeners requested that he make his sermons longer, the pastor replied, "If you practice all I preach, you will find them long enough."

The pastor suggested something of supreme importance, "Practice what is preached." We hear sermons on every hand. Many of them provide substantial food for the soul, but so often we listen and that is all. God says in James 1:22, "Be ye doers of the word, and not hearers only, deceiving your own selves." Merely storing great truths in our hearts and minds is of little value. These must be translated into living if we are to be effective for God.

Those who profess the name of the Lord Jesus are to take their stand for Him and reveal Him by a transformed life. Simply to say, "I believe," is not enough. Actually, one only believes what one is willing to apply to daily living. So often we find that people will argue for Christianity, unite for it, fight for it, die for it, anything but live for it. The Lord Jesus said in Matthew 5:16, "Let your light so shine before men, that they may see your good works, and glorify your Father which is in heaven." The most effective testimony Christians can give to the unsaved is evidence in their lives that they know Christ. Those who believe on the Savior are new creations. If the unsaved can see the Lord Jesus in you and me, they are more apt to believe.

Two businessmen went to special meetings to hear a well-known Gospel preacher. They were competitors. After several nights one went forward as a seeker of life in Christ. The other was convicted but unyielding. As he saw his competitor going forward, he decided, "I will watch him. If he lives differently for one year, I will believe there is something in it and become a Christian myself." For a year he watched the man and saw a complete change in all aspects of the man's life. Convinced, he too asked for forgiveness of sin through Christ.

I wonder how many have come to the Lord Jesus because by observing our walk they were convinced that there is something real in the Christian faith? Many people never go to church or read the Bible, so every Christian is obligated to reveal the Lord Jesus Christ through holy living.

Peter puts it this way, "Dearly beloved, I beseech you as strangers and pilgrims, abstain from fleshly lusts, which war against the soul; Having your conversation honest among the Gentiles: that, whereas they speak against you as evildoers, they may be your good works, which they shall behold, glorify God in the day of visitation" (1 Peter 2:11–12). "The day of visitation," literally, is the day of inspection when the Lord comes for His own at the rapture. Only those who can pass the inspection, having been saved by the grace of God, will live in a way that will make others want to know Christ and be ready to meet Him.

There is so much hypocrisy among those who profess to be

Christians; it is no wonder that many are not interested in our Christ. We go to church on Sunday and sing the great hymns of our faith with enthusiasm and piety. The singing of a hymn should be a deep experience for the child of God. It can be a prayer, a testimony, praise, or an invitation, but too often it is another step in revealing our inconsistencies and lack of devotion. We sing "Sweet Hour of Prayer" and pray for only a few minutes a day. We sing "Onward Christian Soldiers" and fail to get into the battle for God. We sing "Oh for a Thousand Tongues to Sing Our Great Redeemer's Praise" and don't use the one tongue we have to talk to others about Christ. We sing "Bless Be the Tie That Binds" and let the least offense sever it. Many in our churches today have not really surrendered themselves to Jesus Christ.

In Hebrews 3:1 God says, "Wherefore, holy brethren, partakers of the heavenly calling, consider the Apostle and High Priest of our profession, Christ Jesus." Someone has said that as "Apostle," the Lord Jesus brings us up to the height of our calling and that as "High Priest," He maintains us there. We have a calling more exalted than the children of a king. We have been brought into intimate relationship with the King of kings, the Lord Jesus Christ. We are holy brethren, members of the family of God, and this places a supreme obligation on us to live holy and obedient lives.

The Queen of England, when she was a little princess, was asked who she was. In reply, she said, "I am nobody, but my daddy is the king."

It doesn't matter who or what you are, God has a purpose for your life. He wants to make us like Christ. Then He wants to use us to bring others to Christ.

If you are a Christian, is your life bearing a consistent witness to Jesus Christ? Many Christians know how to make a living, but they do not know how to live. They can talk Christ, but seemingly they have never learned to walk Christ. The Christian faith is more a way of walking than it is of talking.

Which is more important, preaching or practicing? Let me answer that from the Word of God. In 1 Timothy 4:16, we read, "Take heed unto thyself." In 1 Corinthians 9:14, "They which preach the gospel should live of the gospel." 1 John 2:6, "He that saith he abideth in him ought himself also so to walk, even as he walked." There are verses in both the Old and New Testaments that emphasize holiness and obedience to the Lord.

Are there inconsistencies in your life shutting out the Lord's power and keeping others from coming to the Savior? Consider honesty, for example.

The Christian should live in such a way that he cannot possibly be charged with dishonesty. He must be aboveboard in all his dealings. We are living in a day when many people no longer think honesty is the best policy. According to an insurance company report, office employees, executives, and salespeople steal more than one billion dollars a year from their employers. And a recent survey conducted at a top-ranking metropolitan area high school revealed that 91 percent of the pupils in the three upper grades practiced cheating. Though the human race has changed its standard of ethics, God has not. He warns in His Word, "Be not deceived; God is not mocked: for whatsoever a man soweth, that shall he also reap. For he that soweth to his flesh shall of the flesh reap corruption; but he that soweth to the Spirit shall of the Spirit reap life everlasting" (Gal. 6:7–8). We may think that we are deceiving those around us, but we can never deceive God. We are told in Psalm 44:21 that "He knoweth the secrets of the heart." Real and effective honesty must come from the heart, not the head.

You are familiar with the saying, "Honesty is the best policy." A policy may be good, but the word also means "a procedure based primarily on material interest rather than on higher principles; hence, worldly wisdom." If people are honest in a given situation merely to create favor or for material advantage, they might be dishonest in another case if they thought they would gain by it.

True honesty is a Christian virtue held before us repeatedly in the Scriptures. David spoke of it in Psalm 51:6 when he said, "Behold, thou desireth truth in the inward parts." Paul said in Romans 12:17 that we are to "Provide things honest in the sight of all men." He repeated almost the same thought in 2 Corinthians 8:21, "Providing for honest things, not only in the sight of the Lord, but also in the sight of men." And again in 2 Corinthians 13:7 Paul said, "Now I pray to God that ye do no evil; not that we should appear approved, but that ye should do that which is honest, though we be as reprobates." This means that we are to do that which is honest for its own sake.

Probably there is no better way for Christian business people to let their light shine for Christ than in their business dealings. What a stumbling block they are if they are not honest. Christian employees are to do a full day's work for their employer. Christians should realize that they do not only work for an employer, but for the Lord Jesus Himself. How it would relieve the drudgery of manual labor if workers kept this in mind. This same realization could lead many of us to give up our careless ways and to render in everyday life a truer, more honest service for the Lord we profess to love. If you are a Christian, are you honest?

We are living in an age when lying also is routine for many. God says Satan is the father of lying (John 8:44). In other words, the habitual liar is marked by a satanical spirit. His lies are prompted by the wicked one. But you may say, I have known Christians who lie. Did they tell lies continually? If they did, you can well doubt their profession of faith in Christ.

All of us know there are some people who *say* they are followers of Christ, but even their profession is a lie. The man or woman who is in Jesus Christ may tell an occasional lie, but there is forgiveness as he or she confesses to God.

Those who obey God and do His will no longer choose to lie. They will speak the truth in love as we read in Ephesians 4:15. But the habitual liar is outside the fold, God tells us. He is among those classified by the Bible as the wicked. He has never experienced new life in Christ.

Christians need to guard against half-truth. Maybe you are not guilty of a downright lie, but you exaggerate or you tell something in such a subtle way that it cannot be classified as an outright lie. Few consider exaggeration in the same class with lying.

A woman came to D. L. Moody and said, "I have a habit of exaggerating. Can you tell me how to overcome this habit?" Moody's answer was to the point. "Yes," he said, "the next time you are guilty of this sin, go to the person to whom you exaggerated and confess that you lied and that you are ashamed and sorry for it." "Oh, but I wouldn't like to call it a lie," said the woman. Moody replied, "If you do not call it a lie, you will never quit."

God says in Proverbs 28:13, "He that covereth his sins shall not prosper: but whoso confesseth and forsaketh them shall have mercy." If you are a believer trying to escape situations with a lie, face up to your problem. Recognize it as a sin God hates and confess it to the Lord. He says in 1 John 1:9, "If we confess our sins, he is faithful and just to forgive us our sins, and to cleanse us from all unrighteousness."

Christians need to examine other aspects of their lives to see whether they are pleasing God and convincing non-believers that they are for real. I would not suggest that all Christians are hedonists, but I have a strong suspicion that far too many practice hedonism. By this I mean they are living for pleasure rather than for God and the expansion of His kingdom.

In a world blinded by materialism, it becomes more and more difficult for God's people to escape the temptation to give more attention to "things" than to Christ.

A party of engineers became lost in the jungles of Africa. Soon their food supply ran out. In their search for food, they found some berries which seemed to satisfy their appetites for days. The men grew weaker, however, and one by one they died. Later when help arrived, there was only one man left to tell the story. The berries were analyzed and found to be absolutely worthless as nourishing food. They satisfied the appetites while the men starved to death.

Certainly Christians need not deny themselves the necessary and legitimate things of life, but John 6:27 must always be kept in mind. Jesus said, "Labor not for the meat which perisheth, but for that meat which endureth unto everlasting life, which the Son of man shall give unto you."

Don't get swept up in the mad world of materialistic living—with one foot in the world and one in the spiritual realm—instead of nullifying the flesh that the life of Christ might be seen in us and the world evangelized in our day.

The Bible declares and history demonstrates that prosperity can be dangerous. It led Israel into idolatry again and again. It ate the foundation from under the Roman empire. Prosperity presents to the earnest Christian a subtle temptation. The spirit of a covetous materialism, which is idolatry, can overtake Christians as quietly as the falling of a shadow across their path. In order to keep up with the current of social progress, they find that a bigger and better job is indispensable. This, in turn, requires a bigger and better office, farm, or factory. A bigger car and home naturally follow, and sometimes even a bigger and better church.

Money itself has no spiritual significance. Wealth means nothing, for it cannot be taken out of this world. Poverty has no claim to merit. It, too, is a transient condition. Our attitude toward the material is what is important. Where on the scales of values do we rank money? Is it our master or our slave? Do we desire it for what we can do for others with it? Is money a first consideration in our lives or merely incidental to our living for the honor and glory of God? The Bible makes it plain that money can be either a curse or a blessing. It is a trust from God. It is something which He places in our hands to be used for His glory.

For whom are you living, self and pleasure or God and the Gospel? I urge you, if you are a Christian, to take account of your real interests in life. Jesus declared in Luke 12:15, "Beware of covetousness: for a man's life consisteth not in the abundance of the things which he possesseth." Our Lord also said in Matthew 6:33, "Seek ye first the kingdom of God, and his righteousness; and all these things shall be added unto you." Let Christ have the preeminence. If you are a follower of Him, live for Him. Then everything you have will be considered as belonging to Him and will be used for Him.

This means your talents too. The Lord has endowed every one of His children with abilities which are to be dedicated to the Lord's service. When they are used along with those of others in the Body of Christ, they become a mighty force for our Savior and His kingdom. If the Church of Christ is to prosper and do what God intends, there can be no shirkers. We have a high calling, a divine appointment. "We are laborers together with God" (1 Cor. 3:9)—a serious responsibility.

Will He be able to say to you, "Well done thou good and faithful servant?" Or are you living for this world only? Many are so busy heaping up treasures for themselves that they overlook their occupation for Jesus. When Christ walked on earth,

He said to His own, in the words of Luke 19:13, "Occupy till I come." Get a job for God and do it well.

Many Christians are not doing any sacrificial work for Christ because they lack spiritual commitment. If you claim to be a Christian, realize Whose you are and Whom you serve. If you are not a Christian, Christ wants to save you. He paid the price for your sin. All that remains for you to do is to repent of your sin and ask Him to come into your life.

Chapter 11

CLAIM VICTORY OVER SIN

There is victory in Christ that some Christians never find. The Bible tells us how sin should not have control over us (Rom. 6:14). The apostle Paul wrote that he would not be controlled by any sin (1 Cor. 6:12). But many who profess to be followers of Christ are controlled by sin. Some have not even recognized that their "habit" or "weakness" is sin.

Perhaps you know that you talk too much but have not faced up to it as sin. Yet God clearly tells us not to be guilty of an uncontrolled tongue. "Put away from thee a froward mouth, and perverse lips put far from thee" (Prov. 4:24). The word "froward" is really the word for ungovernable or uncontrolled.

The Bible has much to say about how we should speak. The psalmist exhorts, "Keep thy tongue from evil, and thy lips from speaking guile" (Ps. 34:13). In James 3:6 and 8 we read that "the tongue is a fire, a world of iniquity . . . set on fire of hell . . . an unruly evil, full of deadly poison." Our most God-like means of expression can be seized by Satan and turned to his own ends. It's no wonder that James also wrote, "Wherefore, my beloved brethren, let every man be swift to hear, slow to speak, slow to wrath" (James 1:19). And, "If any man among you seem to be religious, and bridleth not his tongue, but deceiveth his own heart, this man's religion is vain" (James 1:26).

It has been estimated that most people speak enough in a week to fill a five hundred page book. In an average lifetime, this amounts to three thousand volumes, or one million, five hundred thousand pages. This is a frightening thought when we consider what our Lord said, "For by thy words thou shalt be justified, and by thy words thou shalt be condemned" (Matt. 12:37). We shall either be justified or condemned, receive reward or suffer loss on the grounds of the words we have spoken.

Evil speaking may be speaking ill of one's neighbor. Gossip is in this category and is strongly condemned in the Bible. God says in Leviticus 19:16, "Thou shalt not go up and down as a talebearer among thy people." Yet there are those in our churches who are constantly stirring up trouble by their gossiping tongues. Paul described the condition of women in the early church who were creating trouble because of their failure to claim victory over an uncontrolled tongue. "And withal they learn to be idle, wandering about from house to house; and not only idle, but tattlers also and busybodies, speaking things which they ought not" (1 Tim. 5:13).

If you know something about another Christian, don't tell others about it. Instead pray and go to the person in a kind, loving way. Do what you can to correct the situation.

Paul in his letters to the churches stressed the importance of careful speech, "Let no corrupt communication proceed out of your mouth, but that which is good to the use of edifying, that it may minister grace unto the hearers" (Eph. 4:29). We are to speak nothing that hurts, but rather only that which helps. To the Colossians Paul urged, "Let your speech be alway with grace, seasoned with salt" (4:6), and this means there is no room for sharp, caustic words.

Much trouble and misery have resulted from the uncontrolled tongue. Few of us realize the serious consequences involved in thoughtlessly talking about others. Gossip has separated old friends and brought cruel misunderstandings. It has blasted the reputations of godly men and broken the hearts of saints. It has impeded the power of the Holy Spirit in churches, preventing revival. It has brought untold grief and misery to pastors and other Christian leaders.

The one who speaks carelessly suffers also. Perhaps you've had the experience of spreading gossip or telling somebody what you really thought, and then for days you were sorry for what you said. And even though you went to that person and apologized, it seemed that you couldn't get over what you had done. God says you can keep yourself from this "soul trouble." "Whoso keepeth his mouth and his tongue keepeth his soul from troubles" (Prov. 21:23). Souls have been turned away from Christ because of careless words of Christians, while on the other hand right words might well attract the unsaved to the Savior. I heard of one such case several years ago. A young man, who had started out as a lawyer, got to making money in some big construction projects. One day, just before the concrete was to be poured, a truck driver backed into the forms and smashed them. As the truck driver got out of the truck and came toward the angry young man, he smilingly said, "I'm sorry I broke your forms, I'll come out and fix them on my own time. But, brother, you have just used in an unholy way the name of a Friend who is very dear to me. And I want to tell you, you're missing a lot out of life." He turned and left.

The angry young man was confused and more than a bit resentful. This truck driver, with his limited education, had upset him with his calm reaction to his swearing. The Lord dealt with the young man until he surrendered his heart to the Lord Jesus Christ and went on to go into Christian service, because a truck driver who loved the Lord had spoken the right word at the right time.

God says in James 3:2, "If any man offend not in word, the same is a perfect man, and able also to bridle the whole body." The word "perfect" here means "mature." He is grown up in the Lord. He has advanced in the faith.

Gossip is not the only kind of speech that suggests you are a carnal believer. Some are guilty of foolish jesting, wasting time with the idle throng, enjoying giddy nonsense, echoing their hollow laughter, and delighting in their wicked conversation.

Criticism is another speech sin among Christians. Yet Jesus said, "Judge not, that ye be not judged. For with what judgment ye judge, ye shall be judged: and with what measure ye mete, it shall be measured to you again. And why beholdest thou the mote that is in thy brother's eye, but considerest not the beam that is in thine own eye? Or how wilt thou say to thy brother, Let me pull out the mote out of thine eye; and, behold, a beam is in thine own eye? Thou hypocrite, first cast out the beam out of thine own eye; and then shalt thou see clearly to cast out the mote out of thy brother's eye" (Matt. 7:1–5). If we deal with our own sin and look at our own failures, we are less prone to criticize others. But most of us recognize other's faults far easier than their good points. The story is told of a teacher who hung up a large sheet of white paper with one small black dot in the center. She then asked the children what they saw. All of them said they saw a black dot. Not one mentioned the white paper. Most of us are like that. Rather than seeing the good in others, we see the bad.

Maybe you irritate and disturb people because you are lacking in the love and grace of God. If we could project ourselves into the lives of others, to understand their problems, their heartaches, their weaknesses, perhaps we would be less critical and far happier, too. Consider the thoughts in this poem en- titled "Do Not Judge Others Too Hard."

> Pray, don't find fault with the man who limps,
>   Or stumbles along the road,
> Unless you have worn the shoes he wears
>   Or struggled beneath his load.
>
> There may be tacks in his shoes that hurt
>   Though hidden away from view,
> Or the burdens he bears, placed on your back,
>   Might cause you to stumble too.
>
> Don't sneer at the man who's down today,
>   Unless you have felt the blow
> That caused his fall, or felt the shame,
>   That only the fallen know.
>
> You may be strong, but still the blows
>   That were his, if dealt to you
> In the self-same way at the self-same time,
>   Might cause you to stagger too.
>
> Don't be too harsh with the man who sins,
>   Or pelt him with words or stones,
> Unless you are sure, yea, doubly sure
>   That you have not sins of your own:
>
> For, you know, perhaps if the tempter's voice
>   Should whisper as soft to you
> As it did to him when he went astray,
>   'Twould cause you to falter too.

Anger is another serious sin among the people of God. In Ecclesiastes 7:9 we read, "Be not hasty in thy spirit to be angry: for anger resteth in the bosom of fools."

And again in Proverbs 27:4, "Wrath is cruel, and anger is

outrageous." Maybe you feel that because your temper flares up only once in a while it is not a serious problem. Billy Sunday had a woman say to him, "I have a bad temper but it's over in a minute." His reply was, "So is a shotgun, but it blows everything to pieces."

Frequently a Christian woman requested prayer for her husband's salvation, but still he remained cold and indifferent. He did not hesitate to tell the preacher, when he asked, that the reason he did not respond was that he didn't see anything in his wife's life that gave her victory over an uncontrollable temper. When the pastor shared this with the woman, she felt convicted and vowed that with the Lord's strength things would be different. Not long afterward she placed a new lamp in the hall hoping to surprise her husband. When he came home, he brushed against it accidentally and it fell to the floor and broke into a myriad of pieces. He waited rather apprehensively for the fight to begin. But instead, his wife laughed and said, "Never mind, it's all right. You couldn't help it. We can get another one." A day or two later, when he was late for dinner, she gave him a big hug and said, "That's all right, dear, I know you have worked hard. I don't mind waiting for you."

Before the week was over, he told her frankly, "I don't know what's come over you. Your terrible temper is gone. If the Lord can do that for you, you had better remember to pray for me because this is the kind of salvation I need."

Many Christians get victory over drinking, profanity, lying, and other forms of defeat, while overlooking the deceptive evil of anger. God says in Proverbs 14:29, "He that is slow to wrath is of great understanding: but he that is hasty of spirit exalteth folly." It is important that we weigh every word that we speak cautiously. The instant we speak a word, it is no longer ours. "Be not rash with thy mouth, and let not thine heart be hasty to utter any thing before God: for God is in heaven, and thou upon earth: therefore let thy words be few" (Eccl. 5:2). This verse includes the real source of the problem. It is deeper than the tongue. It is the heart. Jesus said in Matthew 12:34, "Out of the abundance of the heart the mouth speaketh." The reason our words are not pleasing to God is that our hearts are not right with Him. If you are guilty of gossip, criticism, and temper, examine your heart to determine whether you are yielded to Christ. Only one who has fully committed himself to the Lord Jesus Christ can know victory over these sins. Ask Him for grace to control your tongue. Perhaps you are trying to control sin in the power of the flesh when the Holy Spirit must do the job.

The Scripture tells us that everyone who believes on Christ receives the Holy Spirit into his life at conversion. In 1 Corinthians 6:19 we read that the "body is the temple of the Holy Ghost." Since Christians are indwelt by the Holy Spirit, we must be very careful that we do not offend Him. "Grieve not the holy Spirit of God" (Eph. 4:30). Paul lists six things that grieve the Holy Spirit: bitterness, wrath, anger, clamor, evil speaking, and malice. Bitterness here is temper. Wrath is really anger on a larger scale. God says, "Let not the sun go down upon your wrath" (Eph. 4:26). In other words, never go to sleep at night without apologizing to anyone you may have offended during the day. It is difficult to distinguish between wrath and anger. In fact, in many verses throughout the Bible where God mentions wrath, He usually mentions anger. Clamor can be translated "contention." It has to do with those who try to dominate every situation, to talk others down with a view to exalting one's self. Pride is at the root of this evil. Evil speaking is literally abusive talking—retaliating verbally. Malice as used here means "spite," an "I will get even" attitude.

The apostle Paul tells us not only what we should put out of our lives, but what we should permit the Holy Spirit to work in us—kindness, tender-heartedness, and forgiveness.

There is victory, but we must be willing to do business with God. There must be no halfway measures. We cannot compromise. There must be a sellout. Body, soul, and spirit must be yielded to Christ for His control and His will. Then there will be victory.

Chapter 12

GIVE GENEROUSLY

Many Christians are only on the receiving end in their relationship with God. Of course, you become a Christian when you receive Jesus Christ into your life, and then many blessings from God follow in the Christian experience. But you are not to be a storehouse. Jesus said, ". . . freely ye have received, freely give" (Matt. 10:8).

First we are to give ourselves to the control of Christ wholeheartedly. Then we are to give of our time for service to God, and we are to give of our money to the cause of Christ. Many Christians are selfish when it comes to giving to God. When we compare what they give with what they receive from the Lord, it would seem that they don't care very much for the One they profess to love. God says, "Every man shall give as he is able, according to the blessing of the Lord thy God which he hath given thee" (Deut. 16:17). If we were to give in the same manner in which God has blessed us, it would make a difference in reaching the world with the Gospel of Christ.

Some people refer to the tenth they give to God as though

they are sacrificing. We do not give God the tithe; it already belongs to Him. In Leviticus 27:30 we read, "The tithe . . . is the Lord's." The tithe was required under the law.

Others acknowledge that the tithe belongs to the Lord but think that the other 90 percent belongs to them. In Christ, we have been delivered from the law and we have liberty. We are under grace. But Paul reminds us that we are not to use our liberty "for an occasion to the flesh" (Gal. 5:13). One way is in giving. A Christian having experienced the grace of God ought to give far beyond the tithe. The New Testament standard for Christ's followers is not a tenth, but 100 percent. Jesus said, ". . . whosoever he be of you that forsaketh not all that he hath, he cannot be my disciple" (Luke 14:33). If you are a child of God through Christ, He wants *all*. This does not mean that you are to give all you have away, but rather you are to relinquish all claim to it. We are to recognize the true ownership of everything we have. It is not ours, but His. God is not as concerned with how much we give as with what we keep and spend on ourselves.

When we invite a guest to our home for dinner, we do not serve ourselves and our children first. We serve the guest first out of respect and courtesy. As true believers, we ought not to use our paycheck on ourselves and then remember God if there is anything left. We can show Him respect and honor by first laying aside at least a tenth for the Lord's work before we spend anything else.

Some think a tenth is too much. We don't think a tenth is too much when we tip the waiter after eating in a restaurant. In fact, in most cases we leave fifteen percent as a gratuity. Should we do less for God, who gives us all things, than for someone who performs a few moments of service?

Many Christians are not being used of the Lord today because of their desire for comfort and ease. God says in His

Word, "Lay not up for yourselves treasures upon earth, where moth and rust doth corrupt, and where thieves break through and steal: But lay up for yourselves treasures in heaven, where neither moth nor rust doth corrupt, and where thieves do not break through nor steal: For where your treasure is, there will your heart be also" (Matt. 6:19–21). Every cent we spend on ourselves, regardless of how legitimate, is still an expenditure. All that we heartily and faithfully contribute to the cause of Christ is an investment which pays eternal dividends that do not depreciate. What we try to keep for our purse and our person we inevitably lose; but what we willingly share of ourselves and our substance is forever "laid up" for us in heaven. Present blessings and future rewards are God's interest payments on all that we return to Him. Someone has put it this way, "What I kept, I lost; what I spent, I used; what I gave to Jesus Christ, I saved."

It is not wrong to have money. Wealth is not wrong. But the only way to avoid corruption of money, be it a fortune or a pittance, is to realize that you are a steward over what God has given you. Some Christians plan to give when the car is paid for, when the mortgage is clear, when the children are educated. They plan to give, but it is all in the future.

Paul wrote, "Upon the first day of the week let every one of you lay by him in store, as God hath prospered him, that there be no gatherings when I come" (1 Cor. 16:2). In Proverbs 3:9 we read, "Honor the Lord with thy substance, and with the firstfruits of all thine increase." First, we are to "honor" the Lord with all that we receive from Him, and second, we are to remember Him first, before any other obligations are considered. He should receive the "firstfruits." Some never have anything left for the work of God, because they spend it. When God's people put the Lord first in their giving, they will not want for any good thing.

Henry Parsons Crowell, former president of the Quaker Oats Company, gave from 60 to 70 percent of his income to the work of the Lord for more than forty years. He began this sacrificial giving when he came to know the Lord in a deeper way. This is usually true. Those who have a vision of the importance of sacrificing for God have first of all recognized their own need of yielding completely to the Lord. Paul declared, they "first gave their own selves to the Lord" (2 Cor. 8:5). A full heart commitment to Christ usually results in a life of unselfish devotion to Him.

When one gives with love for the Lord, out of a heart of appreciation for Him, God always far exceeds our giving by His provision. It is impossible to get ahead of God in giving. It is somewhat like the African violet. The more cuttings you take from the plant, the more it grows.

You will find the promise of Luke 6:38 to be true. "Give, and it shall be given unto you; good measure, pressed down, and shaken together, and running over, shall men give into your bosom. For with the same measure that ye mete withal it shall be measured to you again."

Perhaps your giving is based on what you have and not on faith. Take a step of faith and tell the Lord that you will do greater things in the realm of giving and that you will trust Him to enable you to do it. Maybe you have not really tested God relative to your finances. Why not give Him a chance to prove to you what He can really do? Don't expect to be able to figure it out. We are to "walk by faith, not by sight" (2 Cor. 5:7).

Some preachers refuse to discuss Christian stewardship from their pulpits, yet Christ spoke about money frequently when He was on this earth. In fact, thirty-eight of His parables were concerned clearly with stewardship of material possessions. Furthermore, do you know that the Bible refers to prayer about five hundred times, to faith less than five hundred times, and to material possessions about a thousand times.

If a Christian is not giving to God in a manner pleasing to the Lord, he or she is sinning. Some who would not think of continuing in some other sin are holding back on God as far as investing in His work is concerned.

Some years ago there was a man named William Allen White. He was a very generous person. One day, while handing the mayor the title of a tract of land to be used for a city park he said, "Your Honor, there are three good kicks in a dollar. One kick comes when you earn it. This I have had. I greatly enjoyed it. The second kick comes from just having it. This I inherited from my father. He was a Scotsman. I have much enjoyed having it. The third kick comes in giving it away. This I inherited from my mother. She was Irish. I willingly indulge in that privilege." Considering the vast needs in the world for the Gospel of Christ, many believers have never come into the "third kick." They know well the kicks of earning and having money. There is joy and satisfaction in these, but the supreme satisfaction comes in giving. The Lord Jesus reminds us, "It is more blessed to give than to receive" (Acts 20:35).

Dedicate your income to the Lord and receive the blessing He has for you. Start taking 25 percent or more of your income for God. Perhaps you are saying, "I could never do that." You don't know what you could do. Even more important, having never tried it, you don't know what God can do through you. Give Him a chance to work.

Chapter 13

CARE FOR THE BODY AND MIND

Is it harmful to body or mind? Christians should be sure they can answer "no" to this question in connection with any life style or habit they adopt. Paul clearly stressed our responsibility to God to take care of the body and mind. "What? know ye not that your body is the temple of the Holy Ghost which is in you, which ye have of God, and ye are not your own? For ye are bought with a price: therefore glorify God in your body, and in your spirit, which are God's" (1 Cor. 6:19–20). Any detrimental habit is sin against God because we belong to Him. We must do nothing to jeopardize the most effective use of our minds and bodies for God. We should be concerned that any habit we acquire will actually build us up physically, mentally, and spiritually.

A young woman was thrilled with the effects of LSD. She had only praise for its effectiveness to carry her into her dream world. Though she was only eighteen years of age, I could detect the detrimental results it was having on her mind.

So much has been written about drugs that Christians are

well aware of their many proven bad effects. The crime rate and the death rate have increased as the result of what drugs have done to people. No Christian can even consider such a habit harmless.

And there is alcoholism—fourth among the nation's most serious health problems, following heart disease, mental illness, and cancer. Alcoholism does not only strike the unemployed and destitute. A news story illustrates this well. A man was brought into a Colorado court on a charge of killing his wife in an alcoholic rage. He had something in common with the judge, the prosecutor, and the defense attorney. All were battling drinking problems. This evil strikes at every class.

Many American adults are heavy drinkers, according to a nationwide survey. A heavy drinker is defined as one who has a drink almost daily, or five drinks in one session once a week. More men drink than women. Most of the heavy drinkers are in their twenties and thirties, are in the higher income groups, and live in cities and suburbs.

Dr. Andrew C. Ivy, former head of the Clinical Sciences Department of the University of Illinois, said, "Radioactive fallout may pose a health menace to Americans, but alcoholism is a more serious one. The dangers from radioactive fallout are guarded against and every effort to protect the public is being made; whereas very little is being done to protect the public from the disastrous effects of alcoholism."

We should do well to consider the wisdom of some of the famous men of the past.

> Alcohol is a poison men take to steal away the brain.   *—Shakespeare*

> Strong drink is more destructive than war, pestilence, and famine.
> *—Gladstone*

> My experience through life has convinced me that abstinence from spiritus liquors is the best safeguard to morals and health.
> *—President Theodore Roosevelt*

It tends to produce idleness, disease, pauperism, and crime.
                                            —*The United States Supreme Court*

It is a cancer in human society, eating out its vitals and threatening its destruction.   —*Abraham Lincoln*

It is distilled damnation.   —*Robert Hall*

But even more important is what the Bible says about the effects of strong drink. In Proverbs 20:1 we read, "Wine is a mocker." It is also the cause of strife, woe, and sorrow. "Who hath woe? who hath sorrow? . . . They that tarry long at the wine; they that go to seek mixed wine" (Prov. 23:29–30). In the next two verses we read, "Look not thou upon the wine when it is red, when it giveth his color in the cup, when it moveth itself aright. At the last it biteth like a serpent, and stingeth like an adder." Further, we see that drinking can be debasing, "They also have erred through wine, and through strong drink . . . they err in vision, they stumble in judgment" (Isa. 28:7). Drinking can also lead to poverty, "For the drunkard . . . shall come to poverty" (Prov. 23:21).

Perhaps you have already been defeated by alcohol, and you would give anything in the world to break this habit which has mastered you. Jesus Christ can give you victory over the drinking habit or any habit.

Smoking is another habit that is a known enemy to health. There is definite evidence that it causes cancer and is detrimental to health in other ways. In our concern to avoid the more obviously harmful habits we may not be exercising care in other ways. Like overeating. Or not getting enough sleep. The psalmist tells about people who rise up early and sit up late. Then deny themselves sleep for purposes of selfish gain or ambition. I think most of us were guilty of this during college days. Many business people live this way every day. One cannot burn the candle at both ends without soon paying the price.

Have you ever realized that sleep is a gift of God? If you have had the experience of tossing and turning through the long hours of the night, you appreciate more than ever how necessary sleep is to our overall welfare.

God gives to His beloved the sleep of a quiet conscience. Peter's sleeping between two prison guards the night before he was to be killed is an example of one who was not disturbed. He was right with God. He was in the will of God. He had nothing to fear. Some cannot sleep because of a troubled conscience due to acts of dishonesty, lying, or cheating. These things and many more can rob one of precious sleep. Others don't have quietness of soul regarding the future; only those who have met the Lord can have this peace and the sleep of security.

Perhaps you have neglected sleep and endangered your health to make money. Or you worry about your business and don't sleep. "But they that will be rich fall into temptation and a snare, and into many foolish and hurtful lusts, which drown men in destruction and perdition. For the love of money is the root of all evil: which while some coveted after, they have erred from the faith, and pierced themselves through with many sorrows" (1 Tim. 6:9–10).

A man of wealth (after he made all his money) said, "As to myself, I live like a galley slave, constantly occupied and often passing the night without sleeping. I am wrapped in scores of affairs and worn out with care. I do not value my fortune. The love of labor is my highest emotion. When I rise in the morning, my only effort is to labor so hard during the day that, when the night comes, I may be able to sleep soundly."

Why should we intentionally ruin our health? God has provided us with bodies, not to abuse and exploit, but to use intelligently for worthwhile endeavors.

An officer wearing the insignia of a colonel's rank called to see President Lincoln. Lincoln listened with sympathy to the man for he knew that he had a record for gallantry, but he also knew that the lines on the officer's face told their own story of long and unrestrained indulgence. He rose up, and as was his habit when deeply moved, he grasped the officer's hand in both of his own and said, "Colonel, I know your story, but you carry your condemnation in your face." The president afterward said, "I dare not restore this man to his rank and give him charge of a thousand men when he puts an enemy into his mouth to steal away his brains."

When we ask ourselves whether or not a habit is harmful, let's be sure to give it another test. Will it glorify God? Paul wrote, "Whether therefore ye eat, or drink, or whatsoever ye do, do all to the glory of God" (1 Cor. 10:31). We might even think what it would be like to have the Lord Jesus in our presence while we are participating in the habit. Could we ask Him to go with us, or would we be at liberty to share it with Him? Would He be happy about it?

Chapter 14

THE SOURCE OF POWER

In an unbelieving world the Christian must be credible. If Christ is to be honored and new believers attracted to Him, the Christian should resemble the Christ he or she names.

God has made clear in His Word the characteristics He desires His children to have and to project to unbelievers and to fellow Christians. In the preceding chapters we have considered these characteristics, but too often the Christian profile is not what God intends. Many find it easy to talk Christianity but not to live it. We may be scrupulously careful in our actions but never say a word for the Lord. We may appear a stalwart of faith but be filled with worry. Many other failings make Christians less than convincing and our spiritual life vague and incomplete. This is too often true because we fail to use the power God has provided to enable us to live a consistent Christian life. Many lack power because they have not first yielded themselves to God. In Romans 6:13 we read, "Neither yield ye your members as instruments of unrighteousness unto sin: but yield yourselves unto God, as

109

those that are alive from the dead, and your members as instruments of righteousness unto God." There is a challenge in the heart of this verse: "yield yourselves unto God as those that are alive from the dead." The Weymouth translation puts it this way: "surrender your very selves to God as living men who have risen from the dead." When we give up our human personalities to the control of Christ, then there can be a remarkable demonstration of Holy Spirit power in our lives.

Whether it was John Wesley, Amy Carmichael, D. L. Moody, Elisabeth Elliot, or others who have been greatly used of God, they had to settle the question of whether they would regulate their own lives or turn them over to God. Had the decision been in favor of self-will, their names—like those of many Christians—would have been soon forgotten. These men and women surrendered themselves to the Lord as those who have risen from the dead. They relinquished all selfish rights to their lives, and they fully committed themselves to God.

James H. McConkey was in the ice business just east of Harrisburg, Pennsylvania, in the day when the industry was dependent upon the weather. Several bad years had put the company in the red. One year a splendid return was in sight when suddenly the weather threatened disaster. McConkey fell on his knees and sought the Lord to intervene. As he prayed, he realized that he faced more than a financial crisis. He faced a spiritual crisis. The Lord could save the ice, but the question was could he have the use of McConkey's life? The answer was yes. God accepted his yielded heart. After this experience, the Holy Spirit empowered him in a mighty way, and his writings have been a blessing throughout the world.

The Lord Jesus declared, ". . . ye shall receive power, after that the Holy Ghost is come upon you" (Acts 1:8). This means that after we are saved, we ought to give God complete control of our lives; then the Holy Spirit will provide us with power to live the Christian life. Niagara Falls is a mighty display of power, and much of it is harnessed by a hydroelectric plant. Similar waterfalls can be found around the world with tons of water pouring over unharnessed. This is all wasted power.

Likewise, many Christians have not harnessed the resources they have in Christ to be witnesses and living examples of His grace and glory. Some are like Samson. He could tear a lion apart, he could easily handle a couple of hundred Philistines, yet this was wasted power because he was disobedient to the revealed will of God. And because of his disobedience, he came to an early death. On the other hand, the apostle Paul is an example of one who laid hold on the power of God and was used as a mighty missionary and a great soul winner. The same power that motivated Paul to go all over the known world is available for every believer today.

The world, the flesh, and the devil are three enemies confronting all Christians. Without the power resulting from a yielded life, we cannot handle these enemies. We have the flesh within us, and among its repeated manifestations are jealousy, hatred, strife, worry, impatience, and many more. We say with Paul, "I know that in me (that is, in my flesh) dwelleth no good thing" (Rom. 7:18). We have the world around us, the system of things appealing to the flesh within. This seeks to provide every comfort and convenience, every satisfaction, every desire of life—educational, social, moral, physical, financial—but apart from God. And then there is the devil who far excels man in position, power, cunning, and deceitful ways, who seeks to make the world alluring and to keep us from God.

Paul described those who are not yielded to God as "Having a form of godliness, but denying the power thereof" (2 Tim. 3:5). As a result, their lives are far from convincing to others or pleasing to God.

We need to lay hold of the promises of Scripture and yield ourselves fully to the Holy Spirit. We need not look for a second Pentecost but only for the blessing of the first Pentecost. It is not a repetition of Pentecost we need but a realization of it. Power is at our disposal. All God asks is that we yield ourselves to His control and turn our lives over to Him. Paul wrote, ". . . be not drunk with wine, wherein is excess; but be filled with the Spirit" (Eph. 5:18). The word "filled" is really the word "controlled." As we drive our car we have it under control. Occasionally we hear of a wreck and sometimes of a fatality because the driver lost control. Very often we hear of spiritual wrecks and spiritual fatalities, not because of the driver losing control, but because we refuse to permit the Lord to control us. We try to live by our own puny human wisdom, making mistakes, creating problems, breaking friendships, all because of living in the control of the flesh rather than the Spirit.

When we do our part, He does His. Ours is yielding. His is filling. He stands ready to fill every recess of our being that is yielded to Him.

A friend told of examining the locks after they were constructed between Puget Sound and Lake Union in the state of Washington. He went down into the great concrete spillways before the water was let through. The water was only waiting the moving of a lever to rush and fill every bit of space where he was standing. So it is with the blessed Holy Spirit. If we are willing to give God control, there will be no limit to the incoming power.

Are you using His power to live consistently?